THE
HEART-
CENTERED
LEADER

The Heart-Centered Leader:
Creating Impact in Today's Workforce and Beyond

2025 fEMPOWER Press Trade Paperback Edition.
Copyright © 2025 Julie Cass

Published in Canada, for Global Distribution
by fEMPOWER Publications
www.fempower.pub
For more information email: info@ygtmedia.co

ISBN trade paperback: 9781998754953
eBook: 9781998754960

To order additional copies of this book:
info@ygtmedia.co

THE

HEART-CENTERED LEADER

CREATING IMPACT IN TODAY'S WORKFORCE AND BEYOND

JULIE CASS

TABLE OF CONTENTS

SECTION 2: AN AWAKENED LEADER'S BEST PRACTICES

INTRODUCTION

Just imagine for a moment waking up every day and knowing that you are creating impact in people's lives that then creates ripples of positive changes in the people's lives around them. This is the influence you get to make as a leader every day, and it is one of the biggest privileges on earth. However, there is one key principle that is needed to create this kind of influence and to make it fun and sustainable, which most leadership books overlook. This key principle is to look within first, to nurture our inner world, our minds, and our emotional health. When we do this it allows us to tune in to our hearts, where our power lies, and we can then create meaningful, sustainable impact and have more fun along the way.

The workforce has changed, and how leaders need to show up has as well. We are in a time when emotional health is needed in the workplace. As a result, what we need out of our leaders has changed. How we need to engage and show up for our teams has also changed, which fundamentally means our leaders need to adapt to thrive.

The emotional health of our leaders is needed to help with the emotional health of our employees. We are living in a time when stress and burnout are at unprecedented levels. We need to address what is missing to heal our workforce. Most books will talk about the statistics of what makes a great leader and how to communicate better and how to engage our employees and other great leadership practices. However, this falls short of what our leaders need today. The truth is, most leaders would already be doing these things if they had the capacity to do so; and for many, it is not the lack of skill or talent. Most leaders forget one key thing—to heal themselves first. They need to look at the emotional baggage that is weighing them down, to look at how to manage their own stress, and to thrive first. By becoming a balanced and heart-centered person, you can be an inspirational and productive leader.

Leaders are humans and need to do self-work. They need healing. Sometimes we are expected to be superhuman as leaders, to be almost robotic, to not have our own problems, emotions, or feelings. This has led to a fundamental breakdown in leadership today and is part of why we are seeing such a high rate of burnout among leaders, more than any other group of people. A 2019 survey[1] of Canadian management found that 96 percent of senior leaders are experiencing burnout, costing companies on average up to $344 billion a year. It's interesting to note that this was actually pre-pandemic, and now we are dealing with even more stressful situations and constant changes and unknowns. Today, burnout continues to be on the rise with middle management reporting the highest levels of burnout. Unless we see a fundamental cultural shift around wellness in the workplace, these costs will continue to rise and have detrimental effects on the overall success of organizations and our health-care systems. A burned-out leader is no good to anyone, including themselves.

This book will unpack all of what it takes to be an awakened impact leader, but first we look at how and what we must heal within ourselves to have the capacity for great leadership.

The first section is all about healing the leader within you. As a leader or aspiring leader this will be one of the most important things you do. This means putting the ego to the side, not pretending you are fine but opening to the possibility that when you can heal within, you can create magnificent impact around you.

Once you learn and adopt the strategies outlined and begin to do your own emotional, physical, and mental healing, then you can approach the second half of the book, which is about putting the new world leadership strategies in place. This doesn't have to feel hard or difficult; in fact, it should feel like it is authentically you—it can be an extension of you, and you will feel in flow.

However, without healing what needs to be healed and nurturing what needs to be nurtured within you first, you will just continue the rat race you've already been on. You will continue the stress and feel like you have no time in the world for all the things you need to get done, never mind the increased demands of the workforce. You will likely keep going until you get a big wake-up call. Because ultimately for most of us, this way of living—having no balance or patience for our loved ones and taking work issues home with us—does not make for a very happy or healthy life.

This is why this book is so important now. I realized a long time ago that I was living by old belief systems that kept me shackled around my career and what I believed I had to do to be a good leader. I used to focus solely on the outside world, meaning I'd work more hours, exceed customers' expectations, be available all the time, work harder than anyone else, plow through problems, and always pretend to have it together. I was focused so much on the outside world that I ignored the voice in my head that was telling me "This is out of balance; this is not healthy," until I could not ignore it anymore.

I want to take the old paradigm that being a great leader means it must be hard, you must hustle, or worse, you must sacrifice yourself so you can be there for others. These beliefs will not work for sustainable healthy success in this time and space. They will always lead to burnout or unhappiness because they create a work environment where we don't foster our emotions and we ignore our body's signals, which will eventually catch up with us. Sometimes the wake-up call is huge. To prevent this from happening, we need to change.

We are in a powerful time in history. A shift in consciousness is underway, and different ideas about what the planet needs are being understood. We are being called to move from aggression to a more nurturing and loving energy. Leaders have the opportunity to make an amazing impact and positive ripples through our planet. Earth is starving for love, for healing, for nourishment; we need more feminine Mother Earth energy to heal and be well. This is also true in our workforce—we need a shift. It is time to lead with the human side first, not shying away from emotions but embracing them.

We need to create psychological safety and a growth culture, not just in our careers but also in personal development and wellness. At this time, we desperately need holistic leadership—leaders who lead in a way that cares for everyone's well-being *and* business results. The most amazing thing happens when we as leaders prioritize a holistic approach to leadership. The results come in, and goals and projections become attainable with more ease and flow rather than force and burnout.

There is a reason why stress in the workforce is at unprecedented levels: it is a cry for help, a call for change. As a leader, you have the power within you to answer this call, to be part of this shift that is so needed. It is time to start living in all moments, which includes work life. It is a time to bring joy into the workplace, to really get excited about work, to feel empowered, and to feel purpose. It makes no sense to live for the weekends, to dread going to work or wish we had a day off, to wish our years away until we can afford to retire. Imagine a world where work was your passion, where you nourished yourself rather than depleted yourself at your job. Where your job could fuel you because you felt passion for what you do rather than consumed with the stress. Imagine a world where people smiled more, were happier, spread more kindness, and excelled at their careers with ease. All of this is possible and necessary for this time on our planet. All of this is within our reach, and it all starts with conscious and holistically heart-centered leadership.

What employees value most from their leaders has changed at a rapid pace in the last decade. We are in interesting times as we have baby boomers who are still in leadership positions that are used to the "old ways" of leading that did not include space for emotional health as a priority. The old-school way was to be quiet and get it done, don't complain, do what it takes. This is how I was taught by my parents and their generation. It was normal. It didn't matter if your life was "out of balance," as the most important thing was to get the job done.

Now we have shifted, and we needed to shift. The most important thing has now become centering emotional safety. How you feel while doing your job is as important as doing the job itself. Studies[2] have shown that most people will leave their jobs for one with less pay if it improves their emotional well-being. We have shifted from rigidity to prioritizing flexibility. We have seen huge shifts in organizations since the pandemic, with many needing to pivot and create more of a work-from-home culture to survive. Now this has become the "new norm" and expectation of employees. It is no longer about a pandemic but a new lifestyle; once tasted, employees don't want to go back to the old ways of working. Companies unwilling to pivot and adapt are struggling. Employee engagement has become one of the most important indicators of the health of the organization. Studies show today's employees won't stay in jobs as long as baby boomers did.[3] Employees change more frequently as they prioritize mental health and well-being more.

This has created a great opportunity for organizations and leaders, if you are willing to create change within and to lead from a place of love rather than fear. The possibilities are endless, and with some simple shifts, you can and will create the impact that is needed. It shows that company culture and a healthy work environment have become more important to retention rates. If, as a leader, you are focused on prioritizing this, you will be ahead of the curve.

This is not just a book on how to become a better leader, which might inspire you for a short time, but kind of like a fad diet, it will not create long-term healthy change. The fact is you probably already know what it takes to be an impactful leader. But to be authentic and implement lasting and easy change, we need to change within first. Throughout this book, I will share tried and tested leadership growth exercises, principles, and mindset upgrades that will help you develop the tools you will need to be a more effective leader.

This book will help you become healthier, happier, more energetic, more engaged in your own life, more optimistic, and more positive, so you can then be the best leader you were destined to be.

Whether you have been leading for a long time, are a new leader, or want to become a leader one day, you will find golden nuggets in this book. Leadership is a privilege, and not one to take lightly. Your health, happiness, and evolution are also a privilege and should not be put on the backburner for work. The best leaders realize they can only take their team as far as they are willing to go—and grow—themselves.

Leaders, it is time to start growing and becoming more aware of the power we all have within us to make great changes around us. If you wait for the world to right itself for you to feel better or do better, you will be waiting your lifetime away. The minute you realize that the real change starts from within, you get your power back because this is what you are in control of. Taking 100 percent responsibility for yourself first will then create positive ripples around you. Not only will you feel amazing, but your energy will lift your team and those who are privileged to be around you.

Leadership is not about sacrificing yourself. It is about bettering yourself to be better for others.

You've got this.

Much love,

Julie

HOW TO READ THIS BOOK

This book is designed with two sections. The first section is all about how you thrive as a leader. It is designed for you to take the time to invest in yourself and nurture your emotional health. The heart-centered leader will always lead with love; and to do this, they must invest in themselves first. There are exercises at the end of each chapter to help with emotional healing, self-reflection, and intention setting to allow for a healthy internal environment, meaning your mental program. The health of your mental internal program as a leader will create success in all areas of your life.

The second section of the book reviews leadership best practices for effective heartfelt leadership in today's world. The workforce has changed, and this section goes over the best practices to allow you to thrive as a leader now. This section is composed of data collected from hundreds of employees and leaders I have had the privilege to train and coach, from some of the latest research studies, and from thirty years of leading my own teams. There are key points at the end of each chapter to reinforce your learning as you continue your journey to become a heart-centered leader.

SECTION 1:
HEAL YOU FIRST

CHAPTER 1:
IT'S YOUR TIME TO SHINE

In life, the emotional healing journey can be complex and layered, but one thing I know for sure is that we are all meant to shine.

As a leader, we must first be radically responsible to ourselves to have the authentic capacity to lift others up. We should never feel depleted as leaders. The only reason we would be is if we are ignoring the messages meant for us, ignoring what our bodies are always trying to tell us, ignoring the inner truth that is always calling out to us if we are willing to listen. When we don't take time to tune into this beautiful navigation tool (inner self) that has been given to each of us, we miss so many opportunities to create with ease, to be in flow, and to radiate and create incredible impact just by being us. Just by being YOU.

So, no matter who you are—a leader of a huge organization or a leader in your home—we all have the inner shifting or the inner healing to do. If you are brave enough to look at what needs shifting or releasing, you can free yourself from the emotional shackles that have held you back, kept you in anger or resentment, kept you in guilt or shame or dreaded fear.

All of this can be released when we do inner work or emotional healing. I know this emphatically based on my own life and those of my clients. I have seen the beauty and magic that happens through Emotional Freedom Technique (tapping) and hypnosis (both explored further later on), through which we can put down the emotional bags that we have been carrying for years. Some of those bags are so heavy and so familiar that we are not even aware we are carrying them. I challenge you to look at the bags you are carrying that no longer serve you. You might be reading this thinking: "I don't have any emotional bags." Or even "Where do I start? I am so ready to let this weight go."

Even if you don't think you have much emotional baggage, you probably do. All of us do. Some might be carrying heavier baggage than others, but it is impossible to go through this life and not have imprints or dents in our armor that have taken us out of alignment. How do you know this? Well, anytime you feel insecure about anything, guilt of any kind, or shame, you are out of alignment; you've moved away from your true self. If you feel your stress is out of balance—meaning stress is a normal state for you—it has become chronic, which is not your natural state. What has pulled you out or made you feel that way?

It could be a comment someone made to you, lack of validation when you really needed it, emotional or verbal abuse from a loved one, or something you did in the past that you have not fully forgiven yourself for. Many times, it is an old belief system or pattern that no longer feels right. Anytime you feel anything less than joy or peace or love, which is our natural currency, it means we are out of our truth.

Now, to feel this from time to time is totally normal. I believe we need to feel this because how do you know the light if you never experience the dark? It is normal for our emotions to have roller-coaster vibes from time to time. The issue is when the negative emotions become so familiar that they are the most dominant. Emotional healing is needed when these lower frequencies have such a grip on you that they are dimming your light, holding you back, or keeping you small in any way. You are a divine powerful being. PERIOD. If you do not believe this for an extended time, then that is your message to release, let go, and be free of the emotional baggage that is weighing you down.

I recommend beginning this liberating inner shift by taking a moment when you feel "off" to get curious as to what it is about. When someone else makes you angry, get curious about what that is triggering within you. When you are judging someone else, get curious as to what you are judging within yourself. When you are feeling guilty about something, question what you are worried about. How are you preserving the actual thing that you feel guilty about? How might it poorly reflect on you?

One thing I know for sure is that no matter what circumstance you come from, or negative things that may have happened in the past, you can heal the emotional wounds that have made you feel heavy or stuck. However, the key here is that the healing journey starts and ends within. It is the soul's journey to release and let go, and no one else has the power to do this for you but you. The good news is that you don't have to wait for other people to get their shit together for you to feel better—you just must take care of yourself, and the rest will fall into place.

The key to releasing what no longer serves you, hence shining your light brighter, is to first identify what emotions are weighing you down. It helps to get quiet when you don't feel good and ask yourself: What am I really feeling here? It is often easy to identify anger as an emotion. I would encourage you to go even deeper by asking yourself what is below the anger or the frustration. This might be the surface emotion you want to release and heal, but usually there is a deeper emotion that we attach to, and it always comes back to our own self-reflection. Ask yourself: What am I preserving to be true about myself in this moment?

Taking this moment to pause and do some deeper self-reflection is essential to lightening your emotional load and getting back to your center.

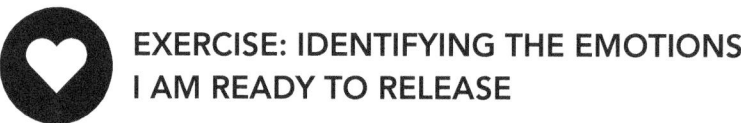

EXERCISE: IDENTIFYING THE EMOTIONS I AM READY TO RELEASE

Identify three negative emotions you feel often and would like to shift. Awareness is the first key in making any change.

1.

2.

3.

LIST OF SUGGESTIONS:

fear, anger, shame, guilt, procrastination, loneliness, rejection, self-criticism, jealousy, sadness, hate, frustration, grief, despair, helplessness, doubt, nervousness, depression, anxiety, boredom, passiveness, regret, lack of worthiness

REFLECTIONS:

Identifying my negative emotions helps me become more in tune with my body and what I want to change.

This is a positive first step in tipping my emotional scale in the right direction. Meaning I get to feel the higher-vibe emotions more often of courage, love, joy . . .

Any program or belief system that no longer serves me can be reprogrammed or rewired in my brain.

CHAPTER 2:
WHEN YOU GROW, YOUR TEAM GROWS

Whether you feel like you were born to be a leader or if this is a skill you want to develop, this book has landed in your lap for a reason.

I have been drawn to leadership since I was young. I knew I wanted to motivate others to be their best, to do their best, and to work as a team. My leadership role started when I began playing organized sports. I was often the captain of the many teams I played on, and I naturally was drawn to wanting to do better myself and to help inspire others to do the same. To never quit and have a positive attitude when things become a challenge. During my senior year of high school, I was the sports head of the whole school. I would get up in front of seven hundred kids every morning to inspire them and motivate them with our daily sports news.

I look back on my first career role as a leader and I felt like I found my stride, my truth, my passion. At age twenty-three, I led a team of over fifty people when we did a multimillion-dollar expansion of our family business to build a first-in-class 10,000-square-foot spa addition to the existing resort. I had never run a spa before and had no idea what I was doing. I remember going to school at night to get my aesthetician license and being at work all day ordering equipment, planning menus, and building systems, all to prepare for the spa to open.

Even though my life was completely out of balance, I had a certain adrenaline rush like I had never felt before. I look back now, and I know it was purpose. I felt a purpose to get out of bed every day, to lead a team, and to make a difference in people's lives by giving them great service and an amazing relaxing escape from their world by offering them a temporary reprieve at the spa. A day of wellness. I look back over twenty-five years ago, and I would give the younger version of myself as a leader so much advice now that I could never have understood back then.

I would have told my younger self some sage advice like:

- Don't take yourself so seriously.
- Remember to have fun.
- Be transparent with your team.
- Communicate to them about the bigger vision of the spa and resort.
- Ask them about their goals in life.
- Find out more about them as people; bring more of your human side to the job.
- Don't forget about your own wellness; you are not a robot.
- And most importantly, I would have said to go deep within yourself. The more you work on you as a person, the further you can take your team.

I can honestly say that if I knew some of the things I know today back in my early days, I would have experienced a lot less heartache. Now, I am not saying the downturns are not important, and in some cases, we need to go through them for our own personal growth. But if this book can help you skip some steps and become a better leader today, then why not hit the easy button?

When I first became a leader in my early twenties, I had a lot of learning and growing to do myself. The biggest thing for me was to figure out my own voice and beliefs over the ones that were instilled or programmed in me from the time I was a kid. As the years passed, my leadership style, approach, and overall effectiveness grew as a direct correlation to how I invested in my own personal growth. My most important leadership role, being a mom, has also changed over the years as I have changed.

It is such a privilege to be a leader. It is a huge responsibility to perform this task to our best, and the most effective way is to invest in our own personal growth. This includes understanding our own triggers and why we have them. Investing constantly in our own mental health. Loving ourselves on a deeper level each day. Paying attention to our inner critic and looking to heal and become our inner cheerleader. Having love and compassion for ourselves. Learning to forgive. Learning to own our mistakes and take accountability. Learning humility. And most importantly, figuring out what the heck we need to do to be happy. Ultimately, happy people make much better leaders.

There are many things I have done over the years—and continue to do—to grow as an individual so I can grow as a leader, and I encourage you to do the same. The best part of committing to your personal growth as a priority is your life will become so much richer.

The world needs impact leaders who create a healthy work environment where people feel safe to grow personally and professionally, where leaders consider the human side not just results. We need to heal as a society, globally, and this healing can begin with conscious leaders who care. With conscious leaders who love themselves so they can love others more deeply. And yes, the word LOVE is important and necessary as a leader. We need love in our workplace. Gone are the days with old-school leadership that avoided emotions and even viewed employees almost as robots meant only to get the job done. Until the 1970s or '80s, emotional health and growth wasn't a discussed concept. There was an attitude of "Just suck it up and get to work." Most people were in survival mode or provide mode, which didn't foster the emotional side of being healthy and happy at work. Well, times have changed, and our employees have changed, so this concept no longer works. Generations of today are prioritizing their happiness and will change jobs easier if they are not happy. Employees are not as willing to deal with a toxic or unhealthy workplace. This is a great thing and more of a reason for us to eliminate the emotional toxins within so we can lead from a healthy place.

 ## EXERCISE: CONNECTING LOVE AND YOUR WHY FOR LEADERSHIP GROWTH

Connecting on a deeper level to why we do something or why we have a goal to do something is like rocket fuel for you on the days when things get tough. Your WHY will get you through the days when you want to give it all up, and it is normal to have days like that. When you infuse your WHY with love, it is even more powerful.

Write down why you love being a leader. Yes, LOVE. It is important to love what you do, and if you don't, then this is a really good time to reconsider if you need a pivot or a change of role. In fact, this is more than okay, it's healthy to do what I call a self-assessment from time to time. That is getting off the day-to-day routine and evaluating the choices you have made in your life to see if you are happy with what you have created. More on the power of your creative being later. For now, let's connect your WHY and LOVE. Take a moment of quiet and connect to this now.

WHY I LOVE BEING A LEADER:

OR IF YOU ARE NOT A LEADER YET . . .

WHY DO I WANT TO BECOME A LEADER?

REFLECTIONS:

Emotions are a healthy part of the workplace.

Understanding why I love leading will help me through the tough times. It will keep me anchored.

Love is an emotion that is needed to heal the workplace, and as a leader, it is important for me to not only emulate love but lead with love.

Employees today are drawn to a work environment where they feel cared for.

CHAPTER 3:
TIME TO HEAL

Emotional healing for leaders is essential. Why? Because you are human. There is not one person on the planet who does not have emotional healing to do, unless, of course, you have reached enlightenment. For so long, leaders have been listening to the programming that says:

"You need to be strong."

"Don't show emotion; they will think you are weak."

"You need to be tough."

"You need to persevere; fight to get to the top."

"Never show your weakness."

"And never ever let them see you cry."

For many of us, these programs have been indoctrinated in us by our family, society, communities, and media for most of our lives. But where did we hear the messages that say:

"It is okay to have emotions."

"Sometimes being strong is admitting you are scared or don't have the answers."

"You can and will have insecurities."

"You are human, and you will have some limiting beliefs that can be healed and that you can look at."

I know I felt so uncomfortable when I started to change my internal program to these more liberating thoughts. If doing this makes you feel uncomfortable, then good. Keep reading, because discomfort means a shift is needed. We all have our blocks, our limitations, or our belief systems that feel icky or keep us out of alignment or make us feel small. We all have our own critter brains that are not very nice to SELF at times. And being told to be strong does not mean we feel strong on the inside.

So, do you keep pretending, do you keep shelving your feelings and emotions? Do you keep burying feelings of doubt and fear? Here is the bad news: If you do, it will keep showing up and, in many cases, get worse or come out sideways.

Here is the good news: You can admit to yourself that you want to work on your own limiting thoughts and beliefs. You can look your fears straight in the eye, and you can begin to heal within and make your outer life easier as a leader. I believe authenticity is one of the most important traits as a leader, and to be an authentic leader, you need to be authentic with yourself. In hypnosis healing we have a saying: "What you resist persists, what you accept transcends." I have noticed this to be true in my own life, that my beliefs follow me, and my experiences are directly a reflection of my beliefs. Rather than trying too hard to change the outside world, which so many of us do, the real power is when we look at what we are believing to be true first and change that if we don't like the way it makes us feel.

The first step to healing any block or limitation is to admit you have one. So put the ego aside for a minute and let's do some of the healing now. This is a process, and if it is one you are willing to take, you will thank yourself because you will feel like things can be in flow. You will understand what it is like to experience peace rather than force. In my own life, and in my clients', I have witnessed profound shifts from doing the following exercise. I have seen people liberate themselves from chronic stress that has robbed them of their joy for most of their life and be able to shift this within a session. I have seen professionals shackled with insecurities about their strengths as a leader move into a confident and secure version of themselves where they could not only enjoy their work more but also their relationships. I have seen people on the verge of quitting because their burnout was so bad who now laugh at the thought of that old stress having once had power over them because now they feel their job is effortless and easy. You can shift and heal any program you want with an awareness of it first.

If you are ready, let's get to the healing.

IDENTIFY THE EMOTIONAL BLOCK OR LIMITING BELIEF

Right now, I want you to think of one thing you repeatedly tell yourself that does not feel very good. We can always identify a limiting thought or belief by the way it feels in the body. If it doesn't feel very good, then that thought you have been identifying with keeps taking you out of your alignment. These thoughts might make us feel stuck or helpless. They might keep us in fear or anger or make us feel guilt or shame. To understand the effect that these emotions have on our body, it is important to understand the concept of everything as energy. Our bodies are made of energy; our thoughts and emotions carry energy, which affects how we feel in our bodies. When we are holding negative emotions in our body, especially over a long period, the lower energy of our thoughts and emotions lowers the energy or frequency of our bodies. This is where we feel "off" or out of alignment to our true essence.

The key to shifting this energy is in paying closer attention to what you are thinking on repeat. A thought you are telling yourself or believing to be true is always linked to an emotion. Think about the negative emotions you identified in the first chapter, then think about the thought that is producing those emotions. What are you telling yourself right at the time you feel those emotions? The answer will help you identify the limiting belief or old program you are ready to upgrade.

Beware that most of us tend to want to change our situation or environment when we feel off. We drain a lot of energy trying to do this as it is usually out of our control. Trying to change our environment to feel better is a flawed concept as it creates more stress and more of the negative emotions we are feeling, and it depowers us. It sucks the power out of our energy centers in the body. Below are some examples.

DEPOWERING OR LIMITING THOUGHTS/BELIEFS:

"If only my boss would understand . . ."

"This employee is being unruly . . ."

"This is so hard . . ."

"Nothing comes easy . . ."

"I must work my ass off to get ahead . . ."

"This is going to take a lot of my time and energy . . ."

Instead, your real power for change is by looking within and identifying what you are saying to yourself about yourself, situation, or event. Then begin to start changing the thought you have about it, and it will begin to start changing how you feel. You will start to change your energy field and you will feel better. The more you believe these new thoughts, the better it will feel. How do you increase your beliefs? You build new neural pathways in your brain. For a very long time, your brain has been listening to the old thoughts that are heavy. They have become so familiar; they almost feel normal. To change, you need to practice patience and consistency, the same way you would change your body or build more muscle mass. You repeat, repeat, and repeat again.

Mind shifts require the same practice, patience, and consistency. Repeat the new thought that feels better, over and over, until you start to believe it to be true. You will know when you believe it because you will feel it in your body.

Try saying this instead . . .

POWERING OR UNLIMITED THOUGHTS/BELIEFS:

"My boss might never understand, but I will always tell my truth."

"This employee is upset. There might be something going on. I can offer support but also know this is not about me."

"I am finding an easier way. I am choosing easy. I believe this shouldn't feel difficult, so if it does, I will look for how to change course."

"Things are as easy as I make them."

"I take inspired action. I create success while nurturing myself and the things that matter the most to me."

"I will devote the time and energy I need to get this done, in a reasonable manner that is in balance with the other things in my life."

 ## EXERCISE: UPGRADING BELIEFS, FIRST STEP

Write down at least three thought patterns that you are telling yourself right now that don't feel good, that feel heavy.

1.

2.

3.

Remember, accepting them and owning the thoughts or limitations is the first step to transcending or healing this pattern.

BODY WISDOM: YOUR BODY WILL NEVER LIE TO YOU

An important concept to understand when we begin to work on healing our own blocks and limitations is the power of your body. We have this powerhouse that gives us messages all the time about what direction to take or when we might need to create a shift. Our body is always giving us the signals we need—the key is if you are ready to listen. If something doesn't feel good, then it doesn't. Your body will tell you. Another key thing to remember is you always have a choice; you either work on changing your mindset or perception about something or you make a change by changing direction or focus.

The bad news: For most of us we have been taught to shut off these signals our body gives us—we have been told to plow through, persevere, think of others, etc. So, we have learned that it is not safe to listen to our body when it is telling us something. The problem with this is that the problem either grows or our bodies create even more disharmony until we listen. But sometimes, we never do.

The good news: You can change this instantly. Become more attuned to your body. Listen to the signals it is giving you. Pay attention to what is showing up and where. We need to remember that we are not just a physical body, we are also an emotional, spiritual, and mental body as well. When we have an energetic kink in the other bodies, it can show up physically for us. This energetic kink can be connected to our thoughts and what we are telling ourselves that pulls us out of alignment. Change your thoughts, change your reality. Literally and truly without expectation.

 **EXERCISE: UPGRADING BELIEFS, SECOND STEP**

Now go back to those thought patterns that you just identified, the ones that no longer serve you, and rewrite them in a way that feels better, that feels more freeing and liberating. That brings you more joy and love and hope just by saying them.

1.

2.

3.

NOTE: To do this, you write them in the exact opposite way. For example, if you have been saying: "This is so hard," you would write: "I do this with ease."

Remember practice, patience, and persistence. The key is to retrain your brain and mind by saying these thoughts repeatedly until you start to believe them. You will know because you will feel better. Create anchors for yourself. Maybe put a sticky note on your bathroom mirror and your bedside table for you to tell yourself this when you wake up in the morning and before you go to sleep at night. Don't give your mind a chance to go back to the old thoughts that don't feel good. Eventually, you will feel this shift and it will feel amazing.

I want to give you a shortcut right now that will help with diffusing a limiting thought; a simple way you can shift this is through tapping.

You can follow along here, and I also include a link[4] in the Reference section at the end to a video if it is easier for you to watch after reading.

Tapping, or EFT (Emotional Freedom Technique), is a way to create an energetic shift and begin to feel instantly better. It is an effective way of healing our emotional wounds by using the tapping points on the body that are linked to our body's meridians, or passageways, through which energy flows in the body, and combining this with modern-day psychology. The combination of the two can remove blocked energy. Any physical disruption or alignment can be linked to blocked energy, so when we have an energy flow, we feel more vital and healthy all around. We will go into more detail next and give a specific exercise so you can begin to use this powerful tool in your life.

Not only have I seen huge results in my own life, but I have seen incredible shifts with my clients over the years. I have witnessed people who were ready to quit their jobs, on the brink of burnout, completely change their life around after a few EFT sessions. I have witnessed phobias, fears, and confidence issues shift through this simple exercise. You can move from a place of self-doubt to one of belief; you can shift from a feeling of lacking worth to beginning to believe and know your worth. I am so passionate about this simple tool because of the life changes I have witnessed when people release the emotional shackles that have been keeping them stuck or small.

TAPPING EFT DEMONSTRATION:

Let's use a common limiting belief that says "This is so hard, or this will be so hard."

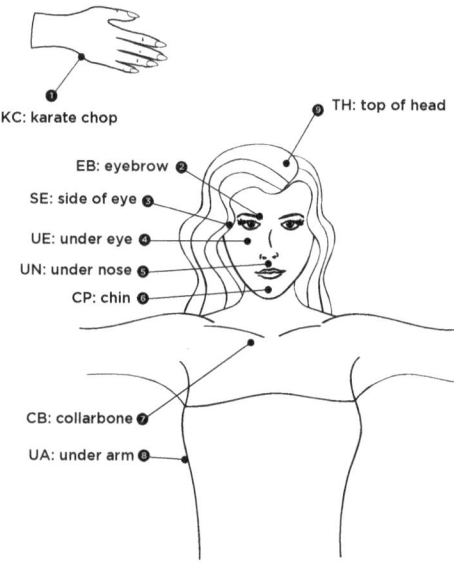

TAPPING EXERCISE TO CREATE AN INSTANT SHIFT:

Set up statement on the **karate chop**: Using two fingers—your pointer and middle finger—tap on the points and repeat the following:

Even though this feels so hard and is creating stress,

I choose to love and accept myself.

Even though I have held onto this belief for so long that everything feels hard,

I choose to love and forgive myself.

Even though I feel like I am working so hard, trying so hard, and it is causing burnout,

I am choosing to believe that there is an easier way.

FIRST ROUND:

- **Eyebrow:** This feels so hard
- **Side of the eye:** This always feels so hard
- **Under the eye:** This feels so hard and stressful
- **Under the nose:** Why does this have to feel so hard
- **Chin:** I don't like this feeling
- **Collarbone:** There must be a better way
- **Under the arm:** I am open to a better way, a better belief
- **Top of the head:** This stress, this feeling of dread

During the first round, we accept and own the feeling, the emotion. We don't pretend or try to deny. That way, we can transcend it and allow a better thought or feeling to penetrate.

SECOND ROUND:

- **Eyebrow:** I am open to a better way
- **Side of the eye**: I am open to a new thought, a new belief
- **Under the eye**: This can be easy
- **Under the nose**: Things don't always have to feel hard
- **Chin:** I like feeling like things can be easy
- **Collarbone**: I am choosing to feel calmer
- **Under the arm**: I am open to believing this can shift
- **Top of the head:** This can be easy; I can make this easier

During the second round, we start to create the shift by shifting the programming (thoughts).

Here is some good news: You can apply this principle toward anything in your life you want to shift. It can be about money, love, relationships, and your health. Whatever thought doesn't feel good, identify it, and write it out. Then write out the opposite instead. Do your own round of tapping to accept it. Then start to tap on the new identity or belief. Tapping will help speed up the process of reprogramming the mind.

REMEMBER PPP: PRACTICE, PATIENCE, AND PERSEVERANCE

Soon enough, you will find that this limiting thought is less frequent. You will find that it no longer has the same governance over you. You will have changed your programming to align with the better-feeling thought more frequently. You will then start to work on new thoughts that take you to an even greater threshold where you feel better. This is evolving and growing. And as a leader, your commitment to others should also be that you will continue to grow yourself.

Tapping is a technique I use daily, and it has changed my life. I will often put myself on an adult time-out when I feel a heavy emotion such as stress or anger. I will do a couple rounds of tapping and can feel my energy getting back into alignment. Then, from a place of balance, I will reenter the room or conversation with whomever, and the results are amazing. We don't get derailed for days; I don't carry the heaviness because I worked on my own emotional baggage.

Once you become familiar with this tool, you will be amazed how easy and effective it is. It's great to use it with your kids, and you can incorporate this into the workforce. Imagine starting your morning meeting with a round of tapping to let go of any stress and have a great day!

REFLECTIONS:

When I feel a lower emotion, the most empowering thing I can do is identify the thought or program I am telling myself in that moment.

Any program, no matter how long we have identified with it, can be upgraded to a new empowering one.

Tapping is a great way to emotionally heal the energy blocks that cause disharmony in our bodies.

An adult time-out with a couple rounds of tapping is a great way to reset and raise my vibration.

CHAPTER 4:
WHAT'S LOVE GOT TO DO
WITH LEADERSHIP?

Over twenty-five years ago, when I had my first job leading a team, my mentors never used the word "love" as a strategy for being a great leader. In fact, it was the opposite. Love might have made you seem too soft. And why would anyone ever speak of using love as a tactic to get results, to perform, to motivate, to reach goals, to make budget, to be profitable?

What the heck does love have to do with it?

If you had asked me this question years ago, I would have said nothing. Business is not about love; it is about hard work. Fast-forward to today and I have a much different perspective. In fact, I think there is such a need for love in the workplace because we are fractured. We are lost. We are overwhelmed and burned out. We are disengaged. Working not only as a business coach today but also as an emotional healer, I have witnessed how the power of love can heal doubt and insecurities and lead to confidence and growth. I have had clients who were ready to quit, to give up, who were able to shift once they moved from a place of self-criticism or loathing to self-love. We are all healers, and the key is to heal ourselves with love. Love is a very high vibration. I teach this in my meditation and hypnosis classes. I can prove this to you right now.

I want you to think of someone or something that you love. Think of them/it right now. Close your eyes and let yourself feel the energy of love as you bring them into your mind. Feel how that feels in your heart center or in your body. Maybe you feel the need to smile right now. Maybe you feel happier just thinking about that person or thing that you love. We don't need science to tell us this; we can feel the energy of love at any moment during the day if we choose to tap into it. So, let's go there now. Let's talk about love in the workplace and why it is needed in such a desperate way. There are two parts to this for you leaders: The first is the need for your own self-love, and the second is the power when you lead with love. The first must be the priority or it will be difficult to do the second part with any authenticity.

GROWING SELF-LOVE AS A LEADER

My leadership style and effectiveness changed over the years. I believe I got better as a leader not only with experience and trial and error, but my leadership growth was also directly linked over the years to my growth in love for SELF.

I quickly recognized that the more I turned the volume up on my self-love, the more I realized my self-worth; and from that place, I made different choices. I woke up earlier and took care of myself with my morning routine before getting into the office on a half-empty tank. I ate better, and I took time for me to replenish. I grew the voice of my inner cheerleader louder than my inner critic. I became more aware of my triggers and what emotional healing I needed to do. I was a happier person when I blossomed my inner love.

My first book, *Me First*, talks all about the importance of loving oneself first. When we realize how powerful this is, we create a bigger impact in this world. As a leader, you have the opportunity every day to create impact. To positively affect others' lives creates more courage, confidence, growth, and evolvement. The most effective way to do this is by going deep within first, by growing the love and admiration you have for yourself. By being proud of who you are and your accomplishments thus far. By focusing on what you have done versus what you have not done. Many of us don't take time for this as we are so busy reaching the next goal or wanting the next achievement. Well, here is the thing: you can be ambitious and self-loving at the same time. In fact, as an ambitious person, it is a great balance to love and be proud, live in the gifts of the moment, and balance this with what you want to achieve in the future.

If we are always goal focused, we miss the gifts of life that are right in front of us. We tend to live in a more stressed state because we are always future focused and not in the present. We are always in a state of wanting and not being. In the present, stress diminishes because we tend to feel more gratitude. In the present, we become more aware of all the good things happening right now.

The power of love anchors us in the moment. Love grounds us, raises our vibration, makes us feel euphoric. The well of self-love is so deep that once you begin the journey of exploring it, you will never stop because it is endless, and you will want more of it. This is a good addiction. Once you set an intention to prioritize your own love for self, then it becomes easier to lead with love. The biggest transformational shifts created by my clients always start with loving self more. Imagine if your inner voice is telling you on repeat: "You are not good enough." This begins to show up in your world; you will get challenges sent to you that prove your "not enoughness."

You will have conversations with others that trigger this belief within you deeper. You might even try changing jobs or relationships to feel better, but you always follow you—and so do your emotional wounds and inner critic until you heal them. The most self-loving and healing thing you can do is look at what you tell yourself about yourself. When I get my clients to repeat or tap on "I am enough" and "I have always been enough," the results are amazing because they raise their vibration from self-lack to self-love. They attract from a different place and their confidence goes up, not because they acquired a new skill but because they started telling themselves a different program—one of self-love. One of my clients has repeatedly garnered the top sales award in her company for the past several years. She did not improve her skill set or get another degree, but she did change her internal dialogue about what she was telling herself. Another one of my clients was able to heal old wounds and patterns of not feeling deserving or worthy enough to pursue her dream job. She is now making more money and loving what she does. SELF-LOVE HEALS.

LEADING WITH LOVE

Imagine feeling good about yourself and believing in yourself and your talents. Imagine being your biggest cheerleader. From that place of self-love, you can imagine how easy it would be to see the good in others, to see others' true potential and what is best for them, to encourage people to step out of their comfort zone and into their genius. To be happy for others' success rather than feel threatened by it. When we feel love within us first, we want this for others too, and that's what makes an outstanding leader. Love heals. It is one of the highest vibrations (emotions) we can feel. When you lead with love, you will get such a better response from your team and your clients, and your organization will thrive.

An opposite emotion to love is fear. When a leader leads from a place of fear, it is because they feel fear within themselves first. Fear of failure, fear of the economy, fear of their boss and their own job security, and that fear trickles down the organization. I have had bosses who have led with fear, always thinking of the worst-case scenario or planning for the worst outcome, and it felt heavy and created a toxic work environment.

My parents came from the baby boomer generation, whose lives revolved around working hard, grinding it out, putting in an insane amount of overtime, and getting results—no matter what. This was the culture in our family business: work consistently long hours or someone else will. Fear was often a normal leadership tactic for getting results. Fear drove people to work harder, to sacrifice themselves, to put their jobs above all else. For years this tactic worked, but it came with a big cost. Eventually it leads to burnout and overwhelm because we are not built to run at that pace for sustained periods. We can do it for a deadline or to get a project over the finish line, but when it becomes the norm or the company culture, it creates a lot of unhappiness because life is way out of balance.

As a workforce, we have suffered as a result. This has led to burnout, stress, and complete overwhelm. Now we need to change fear to love. Love does not operate from a scarcity mentality but rather an abundance one. An abundant mindset is knowing that there is enough for everyone. Gone are the days when leading with fear works to create results. Anytime fear comes up, the best thing to do would be to ask: If this came from love, what would it sound like instead?

 ## EXERCISE: SHIFTING FROM FEAR TO LOVE

Make a note of three things where fear comes up for you the most:

I am afraid of

I am afraid of

I am afraid of

Now sit with this for a moment and feel it in your body; you can even tap on this.

"This fear of . . ." tap, tap, tap.

Then take a moment and connect to love instead. Now from a loving and abundant mindset, how could you rewrite those three statements with full faith and trust?

I have faith that

I have faith in

I have faith

Coming from a place of faith and love will feel better, guaranteed.

REFLECTIONS:

Loving myself first is the healthiest thing
I can do for myself and others around me.

My leadership effectiveness is directly related
to how I love and feel about myself.

Happy people can be happy for others.

Infusing any situation I am afraid of
with love allows peace to rule.

Love over fear is the way to lead for longevity
and happiness today.

CHAPTER 5:
THE POWER OF INTENTIONS

Doesn't it feel amazing to check off an item on the to-do list? Who doesn't love a to-do list? There is great satisfaction in moving from task to task and getting things done. We get a huge sense of accomplishment, which feels so great, and there is nothing wrong with this because we need action to happen to get things done.

However, there are times when the to-do list feels like it is never ending. It can lead to burnout and overwhelm when we spend more time *doing* than *being*. Our society is geared toward go-go-go, the hustle, and how much you can get done in a day. Work culture is all about productivity and return on investment, which is usually measured by the time you spend "doing."

I used to believe this wholeheartedly and never felt like there were enough hours in the day. In fact, in nearly all corporate groups I work with, people say the thing they struggle with the most is time: not enough time for this, not enough time for that, and especially not enough time to take their eye off their never-ending to-do list. The problem with this mentality is that life passes us by, and we get addicted to the busyness so much so that we normalize running from task to task, sometimes trying to do multiple tasks at once. After time, this wears thin because we realize we are working around the clock—and we get burned out. Sometimes we might look for another job to make things better; sometimes we might change our home situation to create less work. But then in reality the same work shows up, the same to-do lists that are never ending, and the same running to try and catch up. The reality is, you take you with you wherever you go, and until you change your ways, it will always be the same.

I chased a different reality so badly wanting to feel like I could breathe, like I could take a break. I even changed jobs and countries to try and find that peace. But nothing will change until you change your own mind. For our outer results to change, we always need to go within first. One of the most powerful changes we can make to creating calm, to being, to enjoying our work life, is thinking before doing. What do I mean by this? I do not mean overthink and create procrastination; instead, I mean get clear on what you want first and then go into action mode.

It's far more productive to start each workday with some inner reflection and thinking or setting an intention of what you want your day to be like. Most of us grab a coffee, start checking emails, and get into the grind before our butt even hits the chair. We don't give our emotional bodies a chance to get into alignment, we just hit GO!

Now I have learned my best days, my most productive and satis-fying days, are the ones when I hit pause, think about what I want to accomplish that day, tune in to how that will feel, and then hit go. This only takes a few minutes, but it is a game changer to how your day will unfold. Getting yourself into alignment is the key. Alignment of how you want to feel. How you want your day to go. Taking a moment before you start your day, think about what the most important things are to get done, set an intention, prioritize, make your to-do list, and then hit go. So, taking time to think before we do gets us into better alignment and makes us take more inspired action versus the feeling of having to do something. This always feels heavy and has a sense of obligation rather than coming from a place of positivity and gratitude.

CREATING AN INSPIRED TO-DO LIST

In my business, one of the first products I created and still use faithfully is my weekly planner for a healthy mind, body, and business. I have always believed that they are all connected, so I created this as a to-do list that is fun and keeps me in balance. I am also a big believer of pen to paper as it creates the mind and body connection.

The following is a snapshot of what this weekly planner looks like:

My clients love this kind of planner because they can do this at the beginning of the week and it sets them up for success, not just in tasks but also in how they feel. We must remember that our feelings are always important. We are not supposed to be stressed and wishing life by. The point is to enjoy it, and that means our jobs should bring us joy too.

The weekly affirmation allows you to set a powerful intention for your week. What is the energy I am attracting?

For example:

"I am vibrant, healthy, and in flow."

"I find joy and laughter in each day."

"I attract my ideal clients with ease and grace."

A weekly affirmation at the top of your to-do list creates an anchor for how you want to feel and what you are creating with intention in your work week. This only takes minutes to think about, but as your week or days go on you can reread this and bring yourself back to your affirmation if you find your thoughts wandering in the opposite direction, such as toward fear or stress.

The next thing I like to do on my to-do list is to separate out three sections:

1. Priorities for the week. These are the must-dos, the things that need my immediate attention.
2. Business-building activities. These are the things that will build my business or portfolio, the growth action items.
3. To-do list. These are all the other to-dos that are important and need to get done but fall into the general category.

When you separate your list into these three sections, it makes it easier to digest, and what needs to be a priority gets first attention. It creates a visual reminder to you of what is important first, and the affirmation anchors you into the emotional part of how you want to feel. This is one of the most important things to bring more joy into your working week. I also love planning my work week on Fridays. This allows me to feel in control of what I have coming up, and it also allows me to really take a breather on the weekends. To take time off to nourish or replenish so I can start my Monday feeling as good as possible. It is not to say I don't ever work on the weekends, because I do, but I like to make this an exception rather than the rule, as it used to be for me.

Living is for all moments; it is not just for when you get home and finish your workday, it is for the minutes and hours that make up the whole day. So, connecting to your emotions and being intentional as to how you want to feel at work is so important. This is the pause; this is the space to think before jumping into do. Get really clear as to what you want and then take inspired action. You will feel so much more joy, less burnout and overwhelm, and a greater sense of accomplishment just by taking these pauses—think then do.

EXERCISE: SETTING A POWERFUL WEEKLY INTENTION

Make an affirmation for your week. Write it out in the positive and affirmative. For instance, do not say I want to feel peace this week. Instead, your affirmation would sound like this: "My week is peaceful and in flow." This is part of that powerful wiring of the brain. You take control and command your subconscious with exactly what you want and what you intend.

My positive affirmation for the week:

Your work week will feel so different when you anchor in a positive affirmation or intention.

REFLECTIONS:

There is power in pausing before doing.
Setting an intention will change my day.

It is easy to become robotic with work and the time
passes me by. When I set intentions before doing,
the doing becomes more joyful and intentional.
The doing becomes more inspired.

CHAPTER 6:
CREATE HEALTHY HABITS THAT LAST

Our health is our wealth, and with an increase in daily stress and demands, it is essential to prioritize our well-being. A balanced approach is to create a healthy lifestyle, meaning it feels natural to want to do healthy things for yourself rather than the inconsistency of radical change through diet and exercise. That does not mean never indulging or giving yourself permission to be lazy, because sometimes that is the best thing for us to do. But overall, our bodies thrive on movement and clean eating.

For most people, inconsistency is the biggest challenge when creating healthy habits. Why? Because you have not made it a lifestyle; you have not changed your mindset around your own personal health and wellness. Most people don't prioritize themselves, so there will always be an excuse as to why you can't do it. For many people, the biggest excuse I hear is: "I don't have time." This is one of the biggest lies we tell ourselves as it is never about time—it is simply about what we prioritize.

This was certainly the case for me. My job took priority over my own health. However, as a leader, especially in today's culture where leadership has become more demanding, we can no longer afford to be inconsistent with our own health. This is one of the biggest messages I spread when I do my corporate wellness talks: How can we create the consistent change we need to be healthy and happy?

I will not get into how to eat right for your body as there are many more in-depth books you can read on this. However, as a health coach, what I will say is how important it is to listen to your body. What is right for one person might not be right for you. As far as movement is concerned, it is important to know that science has proven that movement decreases cortisol, which is the stress hormone, and increases the feel-good hormone, serotonin. But even if you didn't know that and you do now, this information alone is not enough to make you engage in daily movement. There is only one thing that can make you create lasting lifestyle changes . . . YOUR MIND!

Once the mind decides, the body will follow. One of the biggest reasons people are so inconsistent with healthy lifestyles is they have not committed to them in their mind first. Part of this is due to programming, most likely dating back to childhood, where many people take on the belief that you should take care of everything and everyone else first, that you are not the priority. I know I did this for years and always had a scarcity mentality when it came to time. The only way to successfully change my ways was to change my programming. You can do this too.

One of the simplest ways to begin is to change the limiting belief "I don't have time" to the unlimited belief "I am a priority." Then repeat, repeat, repeat.

Reprogramming your mind is one of the most effective ways to create consistent lifestyle changes. This doesn't need to be difficult. Just think of your brain as a big muscle; it needs repetition for change. Hence, repeating the affirmation "I am a priority" will allow you to start believing it is true, and that is when consistent action will take place. From a place of believing you are a priority, it will feel easier to move your body every day, it will feel right to choose whole foods that feel good in your body, and it will feel good to choose things that feel better for your energy and vitality.

DEEPER REPROGRAMMING OF THE MIND

Repeat the new program or unlimited belief as often as you can. This new thought or belief needs to become the most predominant thought to create consistent change. The subconscious mind has no bias, so you need to program it with this consistent belief system of "I am a priority." It will be through inspired action rather than force that you want to do the healthy things that make you feel good. It becomes an extension for you rather than an external part of you trying to achieve something and always feeling like you're failing. You can easily do this yourself; however, reprogramming takes consistency, and creating a new belief will help you propel to a new reality. I see changes happen in hypnosis almost instantly because we get the client into a deep state of relaxation or trance, which makes the new programming much more receptive in the subconscious mind. You can do this yourself with a little focus and practice.

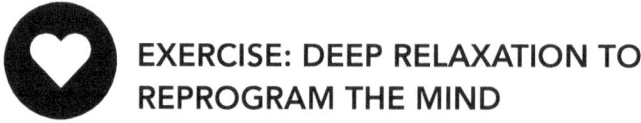

EXERCISE: DEEP RELAXATION TO REPROGRAM THE MIND

The following meditation is to reprogram your mind and create lasting healthy habits. First read through the following instructions. Then give yourself five to ten minutes to do the following:

- Sit in a comfortable position or lie down. Take a moment to get yourself totally comfortable.

- Play soft, tranquil music if it helps relax you. Focus on a spot on the wall or ceiling, bringing your gaze up; don't take your eyes off this spot while you take deep breaths into the belly.

- Slowly exhale longer than you inhale. You can count in for five, out for seven, or in for seven, out for eleven. Repeat this and feel yourself relax.

- With each breath, feel yourself getting deeper and deeper into your relaxation.

- Now, use your powerful imagination and feel your relaxation hitting the top of your head, moving down to your eyes. As you focus on the spot, feel your eyes getting heavier and heavier until you can no longer keep them open, until you want to close them. Gently allow your eyes to close and feel your relaxation moving all the way down to the bottom of your feet and back up to your head.

- Once you feel yourself completely relaxed, repeat the following affirmation in your mind: "I am a priority." Feel what that feels like in your heart.

- From a place of believing you are a priority, what do you see yourself doing? See it like a movie in your head. Feel the sensations of what you are doing in your heart, and how good it feels.

- Stay in this place of feeling and knowing you are a priority for a few minutes a day and you will feel the shift to take inspired action toward healthy habits.

- Coming back, allow yourself to wiggle your toes and fingers, take a nice body stretch, exhale deeply, and come back to the here and now.

TUNE IN TO THE FEELING TO MOTIVATE

Doing this meditation exercise is powerful to create change—and the more you do this, the more normal it will feel to make yourself a priority and take inspired action to create healthy habits. Another way to create inspired action is by tapping into the feeling you get after you finish a healthy habit like a workout or walking the dog. I always say to my clients instead of thinking "I should work out," connect into the feeling it gives you. Let the feeling get you out of bed and be the motivator. Once you do this enough, you will become addicted to that good feeling it gives you.

So many of us are on autopilot that we are disconnected between the actions we do and how it makes us feel. The more we connect into the feeling, the more we get connected to that inner GPS system we all have, and we will be navigated with more ease to feel great. This is how you create the consistency for a healthy lifestyle rather than struggle and force.

REMINDER: INCORPORATE MORE FEEL-GOOD ACTIONS INTO YOUR LIFE.

Here are some of my examples for inspiration:

- Walk
- Move my body
- Connect with people who make me feel good
- Be discerning about where I spend my time
- Create time for quiet
- Rest
- Eat healthily
- Cook

Take a moment now to make a list of all the things that feel good to you. What are some of the things that when you do them you feel peace, you feel energized, you feel like you are more in your alignment? The things that give you power versus drain your power? Just by taking a few moments here to make a mental note or write down the things you love to do will activate your brain and remind you that you get to choose more of these things in your day, your week, your month.

 ## EXERCISE: MY FEEL-GOOD LIST

Write down the things that make you feel good that you are now making more time for:

-

-

-

-

I have noticed in my own career as a leader of large or small teams, my leadership capacity was directly linked to my capacity to make myself a priority. The days I made time for me were much easier days at work, running a business and leading a team. My capacity and coping mechanisms expanded in direct relation to taking time for me. In the beginning of my leadership career, I felt so fragile and moody. If something went wrong with a team member or client, it would rock my boat. I would struggle and live in a place of fear. I was fragile because not only was I running on adrenaline, but I did not fill my healthy habit cup, which made me operate from a lack mentality. Today, there is no way I would trade in self-care. For what? Nothing is worth feeling stressed versus empowered and happy.

As a leader, if you want to create your biggest impact, you will reprogram your mind to become a priority and teach others to do the same. They will get the best version of you, and you will get the best version of them.

REFLECTIONS:

Creating healthy habits becomes easy and natural when I change my mind first, meaning upgrade my internal programming to believe "I am a priority."

I am the only one who can decide I am a priority and make myself a priority—no one else can do this for me.

The healthier I am mentally, spiritually, and physically, the healthier I am to lead a team, have capacity for the unexpected, and have the energy to inspire others.

CHAPTER 7:
THE POWER OF HEALTHY ROUTINES

One of the best ways to create healthy habits and get into a positive and healthy state of mind is by creating a morning routine to start your day off right and ending your day with an evening or pre-bed routine to not only achieve better sleep but also to ease the mind for the next day. Bookend your days with the good.

Our subconscious mind is most receptive to the messages we tell it when we are winding down for the day or when we are in the waking state. This is because we are in more of that trance state; like when we put people in hypnosis, they become more receptive to positive or negative messaging.

The problem with most of us is we have built a habit of letting our critter brain, or thinking mind, run wild before bed and first thing in the morning. Many of us go over our to-do lists for the next day while trying to fall asleep, which is the opposite of relaxing. Or many of us begin to worry about our day and what we need to accomplish when we're first waking up, and we begin to feel dread before our feet even hit the floor. So, we often start our day from a place of feeling depleted, and we bring that energy into our day. It has a huge effect on our mental capacity and well-being. Similarly, at night, we often find ourselves being over-stimulated or exhausted and we go to bed with busy heads because we have not given our bodies and minds a chance to wind down. I always tell my clients if you are going to make one powerful positive change in your life it should be how you start and end your day.

 ## EXERCISE: MENTAL DIALOGUE UPGRADE

So, let's upgrade the dialogue you tell yourself right now.

One of the simplest ways to do this is with the words you first say when you come into a waking state. The following statement is so simple yet powerful, and I have had so many people tell me that just by saying these three simple words, it has changed the way they feel about their day, and their happiness meter goes up.

Those three simple words are: **I GET TO . . .**

For most of us, we wake up and the critter brain starts saying I **have to** do this, I have to do that, how am I going to have time for this . . . Sound familiar? Just a simple upgrade when you wake up tomorrow is to pause and tell yourself, "I get to . . ." and fill in the blank.

This simple word change is so powerful and will instantly shift your vibration and energy to feeling excited and grateful before you start your day. Three simple words can change dread to excitement. "I get to" creates a state of gratitude and shifts your energy.

It can be as simple as this: "I get to get up and move my body, have a glass of water, enjoy my coffee, take a warm shower, choose my outfit, go to the office, do a keynote today."

"I get to" feels so much better than saying "I have to."

When we reframe it in a positive light, it is a reminder of how privileged we truly are. This is a great thing to do right before you get out of bed because it will also create inspired action from a place of gratitude to enjoy a nice morning routine. Your morning routine does not have to be long or complicated, but what is important is that you take a moment to be present and connected before getting into the action mode of "work."

I recommend making a list of the nonnegotiables. What are the things that are the most important to you? This is how you build a morning routine.

I get to:

Some of mine are:

- ✓ My morning lemon water
- ✓ My coffee
- ✓ My workout
- ✓ My meditation

Many of my most successful clients and top leaders in organizations have all said they have a morning routine. One of my clients writes his intention for the day in his journal every morning—what a powerful way to start your day. He gets really clear on what he wants for the day. It can be joy, connection, meaningful conversations, and productivity. You name it, but intentions are incredibly powerful to a conscious creator, and when you make it a morning routine (when you are more receptive to this messaging), it is like you supercharge these intentions.

Make a list for yourself. What is realistic for you? Meaning what can you commit to yourself and follow through? Even if you do this for thirty days, you will begin to build the muscle that says "Hey, I want this. It feels good." And it will become an extension of you. As leaders, when we are consistent with our morning routines, our capacity for our day increases. Not only do we find ourselves more patient with our kids and team, but it also becomes easier to roll with the punches or challenges with more ease and grace. Because our cups are full, we have the capacity for perspective, and our stress levels are manageable, which is one of the most important things to a healthy lifestyle.

BEFORE YOU GO TO SLEEP, SET YOURSELF UP FOR SUCCESS

You know how important sleep is because you can feel the difference in your own body when you sleep. Not only does it allow for more mental clarity, but it's also vital for our body to restore, regenerate, and heal. Rest is essential, yet we tend to do the opposite to induce a great night's sleep; we don't set ourselves up for sleep. If you have kids, you most likely had a bedtime routine for them when they were babies. You started to signal their body and mind that sleep was coming. Sometimes you would give them a bath, a warm bottle, a massage, or maybe play peaceful lullaby music. The last thing you would do is put your baby in front of a TV or screen and then try and put them to bed. It isn't logical. So why do we do this for ourselves and expect different results?

I see many clients with sleep issues, and stress is usually at the core. However, we cannot expect great sleep results if we do not set ourselves up for success. A great nighttime routine will start to signal the body it is wind-down time.

Think of three things you can do to adopt a healthy before bed routine. Try this for thirty days and see how you feel.

Some of my favorites are:

- ✓ Nighttime walk
- ✓ Cup of sleepy tea
- ✓ Warm bath with Epson salts and essential oils like lavender
- ✓ Meditation
- ✓ Breathing exercise
- ✓ Gratitude journaling or reflections on my day
- ✓ Reading a really good book
- ✓ Tapping out any stress from my day

 **EXERCISE: MY NEW A.M. AND P.M. ROUTINE**

My a.m. routine:

My p.m. routine:

Commit to what makes you feel relaxed. Turn off your device and give yourself permission to unplug and unwind before bed. You will be amazed at the difference you feel. Another powerful thing I have used for myself, and my clients, is the power of the mind and programming your brain for sleep. While getting into bed tell yourself, "My body knows how to get into a deep sleep. I sleep through the night peacefully and wake up at _____." I have fun with this and am amazed at how accurate it is. I never set an alarm clock unless I must get up before five for an early flight or TV segment. Literally program your mind before getting into bed. Guaranteed most of you who have trouble sleeping are also confirming this in your mind every night by saying something like "I hope I don't wake up in the night" or "I am so tired; I better be able to fall asleep." You are coming from fear when you do this, and at times, it can create more stress, which causes more lack of sleep.

I had a client who was going through a hard time in her life, and she couldn't sleep. She started taking a natural sleep aid that helped her fall asleep. Life was better because the pill helped her sleep. But when the pill was suddenly taken off the market and no longer available, she went into full panic. "If I can't sleep, I will not be able to cope with my day. I can't bear the thought of not sleeping," she said.

We worked through a series of deep breathing exercises and a new program. I advised her, "Before bed, I want you to tell yourself, 'I am an amazing sleeper. My body knows what to do, and I sleep peacefully and soundly through the night.'" I told her to repeat this over and over like a mantra in her head.

She was amazed at the results, and to this day she is an incredible sleeper, which has also changed her capacity to manage her stress. Never underestimate the power of the story you tell yourself. I share some helpful sleep hypnosis meditations[5] in the References at the end of the book.

Think of your day as your favorite books on your shelf, and think of your morning and evening routine as the bookends to that day. The bookends hold and support your story or your day. How you set up your day and support your day matters. A morning and evening routine is your bookend—it will help support your best, most magical story.

REFLECTIONS:

*An a.m./p.m. routine is like a bookend
supporting my story or day.*

*Our subconscious mind is the most receptible to messages when
we are in the waking and sleeping state; this is like a trance state.*

One of the best things to say when waking is "I get to . . ."

*One of the best things to tell myself before sleeping is
"I will have a great night's sleep tonight.
My body wakes at ___."*

*Never underestimate the power of my internal program
and what I tell myself.*

*The most successfully happy leaders
have a morning routine before starting their day.*

CHAPTER 8:
LOOK AT YOUR TRIGGERS

The ego rears its ugly head for all of us from time to time, and it creates a lot of stress and disharmony, not only for you but also for your team. One of the most healing things you can do for your own self-growth is recognize when you are operating from ego. First of all, it will never feel good, and you can never be as effective and impactful as a leader when you are in ego. Whenever you feel that you need to do it all yourself, you are acting from a place of self-serving rather than team- and company-serving—this is acting from ego. If you ever feel threatened by someone else's success, you are in ego. If you feel like you have no control over the situation, you are in ego.

Ego has complex meanings for many people and can often be misconstrued. The fact is, we all have an ego, and we are all "I." The issue with ego is when we operate from the "I," that is disconnected to our higher self or universal mind, we are separate from others. For the purpose of this chapter and for the purpose of being a mindful leader, we are going to use the term "ego" in the sense of the ego self that is pulling you away from alignment with your true self. This can relate to egoism or egotistic behaviors as well.

The following image portrays the difference of how we see the world from states of ego self or higher self:

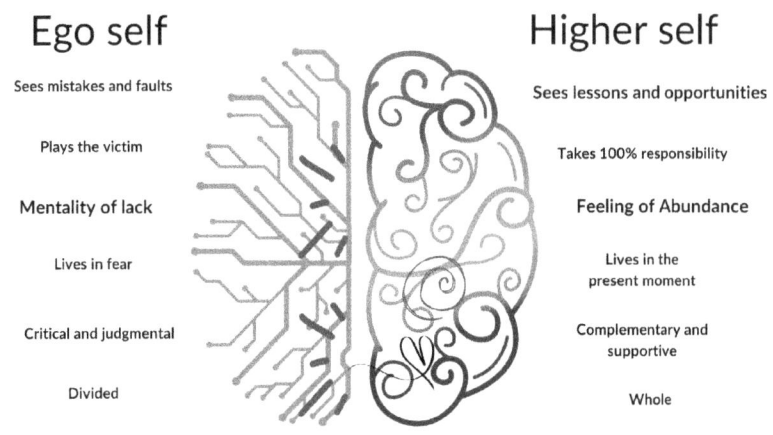

Ego self

Sees mistakes and faults

Plays the victim

Mentality of lack

Lives in fear

Critical and judgmental

Divided

Higher self

Sees lessons and opportunities

Takes 100% responsibility

Feeling of Abundance

Lives in the
present moment

Complementary and
supportive

Whole

Ego connects to the limited self or limited identity we have of ourselves. It creates a sense of separation. Higher self connects to the unlimited universal mind we are all connected to and part of; therefore, it creates a sense of wholeness and inclusiveness as it does not see separation. I would like you to connect this back to how you are feeling as a barometer to know what state you are operating from as a leader and as a check-in to how you show up every day.

If you ever feel threatened by others' smarts, looks, talents, or abilities, then you are in ego.

If you feel a sense of elation for others' success and happiness, then you are in higher self because we are all connected, and their happiness makes you happy.

Now imagine bringing this awareness into your workplace or your home. You will automatically be operating from a different state of awareness, and this will always connect back to your triggers. When you are feeling a trigger or the internal "grr," hit pause. Ask yourself where this is coming from and what it is bringing up in you. If you are acting out of fear, you are in ego. If you're acting out of faith or a peaceful place, you are in higher self, which is more connected to true self.

Let's talk about how we can begin to heal our triggers that arise repeatedly and then we will go into examples of how to incorporate higher-self energy into your everyday. You will be that leader who people are drawn to and inspired by, and you will grow. To create that kind of leadership impact, it is important to heal the parts within that are triggered and keep you in ego.

In my own hypnotherapy practice and consulting with some of the top hypnotherapists in the world, I have witnessed that 99 percent of the problems are never actually *the* problem. The problem always comes from our own reflection of self and shows up in self-worth or self-love. For instance, if we get angry and stressed because our team members are not performing or meeting expectations, it is understandable to get upset, right? Your first reaction would be to get mad at your team. However, there is always an opportunity to go deeper, to dig a little more as to what the problem is about because it might not be about THEM at all. Chances are your anger might come across because of how your team's performance reflects on you. You don't want to look bad or come across as not performing, so your output is anger toward others. This is what I mean when I say that the problem is never actually the problem; 99 percent of the time it is a reflection of our own self-worth that is the true problem.

If you took that same example of your team not performing well, but this time you were connected to your higher self, you might feel disappointed, but you wouldn't project the problem on your team. Instead, you would look at it from a broader perspective. You would get curious about what went wrong: Was it a communication error? Is my team not set up for success in some way? Do I need to look at the systems in place? You would look for the opportunities to create positive changes rather than turn to anger as an initial response.

It is so simple, really; every time you get triggered, hit pause and ask, "What am I making this to mean about me?" The answer always comes back to self; it always starts within first. The irony of ego is we need to go back to the "I" or the ego to heal and operate from the collective "we" or higher self. This is called taking radical responsibility as a leader. Radical responsibility to create impact and change always must start within. The most amazing part of the leadership growth journey is it is a beautiful opportunity for an amazing personal growth journey. You will be presented with so many opportunities to look at your triggers as they will come up. Look at it through the lens of what is this bringing up in me? What can I heal within to be a better leader?

So, to move from ego, pay attention to what emotions you are feeling. They will always be your guide. When you are in hate, anger, or fear, you are in ego. When you are in insecurity, which is a hard one for most of us to admit, you are in ego. Remember, the best way to create any change is awareness first. Being truthful with self, being vulnerable with self, allows you to look at your part in the role that is playing in your movie. How is your ego contributing to what is going on?

If you have the courage to do this, I promise you, not only will you become a more impactful leader, but the results in you and your team's performance will show. And you will just feel better overall about life itself. This requires great strength to look at our shit to shift, and you are reading this book because you are curious enough to try.

EXERCISE: BECOME AWARE OF TRIGGERS AND MOVE FROM EGO TO HIGHER SELF

Make a list of three common emotions you most feel when you are triggered.

Example:
1. Anger
2. Shame
3. Feeling of not being enough

Now look at those emotions and write down a healing affirmation whenever you feel those emotions.

Example:

If my trigger is anger, my anger might be coming from a place of not feeling validated.

The healing affirmation would sound like this:

"My voice matters; what I have to say is important."

LEADING WITH THE HIGHER SELF

When we open ourselves up to the magic around us, we begin to see the miracles that are always happening.

Like I mentioned before, we have duality in every moment, and we also have choice in how we see things. When you see things through a divine lens or from the higher self, you will see all the miracles around you that are happening all the time. When something does not go to plan, you trust that it is still working out for you. You resonate with the ebbs and flows of life making life easier and happier. When you live in ego, you see nothing as a miracle and that you must do the heavy lifting. Bringing higher-self energy into the workplace will allow you to see things with divine flow and trust. Instead of stressing and creating more stress, you will be more in flow and allow pivots and opportunities to present themselves. Everything feels better when we see and feel and allow the miracles around us to unfold.

LESSONS AND OPPORTUNITIES

When we live from the higher self and things don't go the way we want or we find ourselves in challenging times, the best thing to do is pause. Take a time-out, do some deep breathing or meditation, and repeat to self: "I trust that everything is working out. I allow the answers to come to me. I look for the opportunities this is presenting."

I was out with my friend recently and two of his businesses just had the worst year ever and lost money. He found himself miserable and in the biggest funk that he couldn't shake. It brought up all kinds of fear for him, which is totally understandable because as a leader, he took on big risks to grow his businesses, and the economic climate has not been favorable this past year. He started questioning his own capabilities and internalized this as a direct reflection of himself. In a kind and loving way, because we have that kind of relationship, I told him to get his head out of his ass. I asked him where that confident person I knew was. Now, I do not think confidence is the same thing as egotistical at all. In fact, it is important to distinguish and not confuse the two. We need confidence in self and others. Confidence is belief in your capabilities, your dreams, and your aspirations. Ego is when you feel you are the only one making it happen. There is a huge difference.

Back to my point, I looked him dead in the eye and said, "This is temporary. You know how to ride the storm out, and when you pull yourself way up and out of the drama, you know you are okay, don't you?"

He agreed and instantly shifted, as he was in ego. He was in fear rather than faith. I also asked him to look for the lessons, as there always are some, and in a few months or at the end of the year, he would also be able to say the opportunities it created and hence the blessings. We never want to linger in ego as it creates disharmony. The quicker we can lean into higher self, the quicker we can trust and ride the wave.

We will all have moments when our world is rocked, our confidence is shaken, and as a leader you need to be your biggest cheerleader so you can do the same for others. First, believe in self, then when you can, extend that belief to someone else. Put fuel on their fire, wind in their wings, and you will see the magic unfold.

REFLECTIONS:

*Opportunities for growth, self-reflection,
and remembering who I really am are always there.*

The harder times are always for us and not against us.

Believe in my SELF first and I can believe in others.

*Allow others' success to fuel my own happiness.
WE are all connected.*

*Difficulties are never a reflection of me as a person,
but simply a reflection of what I am perceiving
to be true about the situation.*

*When in challenges, hit pause,
bring myself to the present moment, and remind myself:
"I've got this; I can trust everything is working out."*

*Don't see myself separate from my team
but as a part of and connected to them.
Their success is my success.*

CHAPTER 9:
SKYROCKET YOUR CONFIDENCE

Being a fearless leader has a nice ring to it, doesn't it? Let me ask you this: Would you have more confidence in a leader who is scared or fearless? I am sure you would answer fearless. I know I would. We need to be fearless leaders, but that doesn't mean that you will never feel fear. It just means that fear is not your dominant emotion when leading. Your team will feed off your confidence. You can only give others reassurance when you feel sure of yourself. Being a fearless leader means you are willing to stretch the boundaries; it means you are willing to believe in what others think is impossible; and it means you believe that as a team you can make anything possible because you also believe in yourself.

MOVE FROM FEAR TO FEARLESS

I work with a group of healers in an organization called Hypnosis Healers.[6] Through a serendipitous series of events we all met and connected to form a group, in which we put together transformative healing retreats. Right from the formation of our company, my teammates coined me the "fearless leader." I remember at the time laughing this label off and not thinking much about it. But my colleagues kept reminding me of my role and how important it was, and that our company wouldn't exist without me. They also told me they feed off my confidence, which allows them to believe in the magic of what is possible and, most importantly, to believe in themselves.

It made me reflect on my own journey over the years and how I have always stepped into the role of fearless leader. Whether I knew the answers or not, it didn't stop me or slow me down—it just made me more curious to find the solutions and see the opportunities. As a leader, I also knew that one of the most important things to make anyone a fearless leader is to be authentic and real, and sometimes that means looking at your emotions, owning your triggers, and fearlessly be willing to do the internal work to shift yourself when needed.

When you have confidence, you can attract and see the opportunities in front of you. When you have confidence, you can lend that confidence to your team so they can believe in themselves. When you have confidence, you can take yourself out of the equation and see what others are also capable of, even before they can. This is what makes an inspiring and magnetic leader.

As we distinguished in the previous chapter, do not mistake confidence with ego. And for you women out there, please do not mistake confidence for being "bitchy." And if someone accuses you of that, just reject that answer. Literally say, "No, I reject that. I am confident, and there is a difference. Confidence is key in leadership, because the opposite is fear and insecurity, and it is impossible to create a high-performing team if you are operating from these low vibrations."

How do you raise your vibration to be confident or fearless?

If I were writing this book years ago, my answer to this would have sounded like: You need experience, you need practice, you need to prove yourself first, then you can be confident.

Well, this might be true for some. For others, it can take years of experience and a proven track record, and you can still doubt yourself or criticize yourself and not have confidence. You can also have won many times but still fear failure. So, these things do help, but they cannot on their own create confidence. Now, years later into my own personal growth and leadership journey, I believe confidence is directly linked to having a strong sense of self. Meaning you are connected to who you truly are. You do not identify with what others think of you or have said about you but rather the deeper knowing of who you are and your connection to the beautiful, all intelligent universal mind. You can look at others whom you admire in awe, and instead of saying, "That could never be me," you look at it as inspiration and you say, "Anything is possible. What do I want to achieve?" You get really clear on it. And then you say, "I come from that same universal intelligence, so I know and believe I can create this for myself." Every time you keep going back within, digging the inner well deeper to know yourself, you will increase your confidence.

Most of us look to the outside world to find validation and build our confidence. You have probably felt beaten down by life at times. I know I have. I have wanted external validation to feel good about myself. However, sometimes the people we want or feel we need validation from have their own demons or insecurities they have not dealt with, so they could not possibly give you what you need. This is never about you but about them and where they are in their own recognition of self. This is why the most powerful leadership healing you can do is to connect within, build and know your value, be confident, and share this ripple of confidence and belief with those around you. This will make you an outstanding leader—a heart-centered leader.

When things don't go as planned and you feel fear trickling in, you are better off hitting pause than hustling. In the quiet, you can realign to your true self. Raise your vibration from fear to faith and pivot, shift, or see other opportunities right in front of you. When you pause, it is like putting on a new pair of glasses, enabling you to see what is in front of you with more clarity. Fear fogs the lenses.

Does practice build confidence? Of course it does. But believing in your worth and capabilities before you start will skyrocket your confidence more than years of grueling work. I remember the first time I did a TV interview, I was nervous as heck. Now I have done so many that I don't get nervous but excited. So yes, my confidence has increased, and my nerves decreased through practice, like building muscle. However, in the first interview, I still had confidence mixed with some nerves. This is perfectly okay. The reason I was able to give a great interview my first time was because of a list of things I did to prep my mental state and vibration.

My confidence checklist:

- ✓ I became my biggest cheerleader by telling myself: "What I have to say is important."
- ✓ I mentally rehearsed my interview. I ran the tape in my head and took myself right to the end when the interview was over, and I was getting handshakes and thank-yous.
- ✓ I imagined a viewer reaching out to me because of what they heard me say and how it helped them.

✓ I practiced my notes, but I also allowed the messages to flow through me about what I wanted to say. I let myself be divinely guided. This happens in the quiet, in the pause.

The most interesting thing happened after that. All of what I imagined came true. I got multiple interviews with the same station, and I had a client who is still with me today reach out for my services. And the best part, I loved and still love doing them. So, confidence is definitely something that can be built over time, but there are things you can do right from the start to build your confidence and trust in your own capabilities rather than trying so hard to prove yourself to others to feel confident, because this will never satisfy. Prove to yourself instead. Be your biggest cheerleader in the good and the tough times. If you can practice this and do that for yourself, then just think of what you will be able to see in your team or your kids. You can lead from a place of compassion, kindness, and empathy when you have confidence. You can be confident and kind. That is magic.

YOUR BUILDING-CONFIDENCE CHECKLIST:

✓ Look within versus out for validation.

✓ Sit in the stillness and connect to self.

✓ Remember, you are part of the universal intelligent mind, and what is possible for the person you most admire is also possible for you.

✓ Mentally rehearse something you are nervous about, take yourself to the end and see the brilliant outcome, feel it in your body.

✓ When fear trickles in, tell yourself, "This is all working out for me; I trust the process."

- ✓ Becoming a fearless leader will skyrocket your team's confidence in yourself.

- ✓ Ego and confidence are very different. Ego means you do it alone; confidence means you understand you have the universe as your guide.

- ✓ Confidence is simply believing in yourself and the universe you are part of. It means you are connected to Self.

- ✓ Remember, the more you train your brain to let go of fear and feel confidence, the faster this will become more normal to you than fear. You will strengthen this new programming and dull out the old programming.

GREAT CONFIDENCE-INVOKING AFFIRMATIONS:

The key to affirmations is not just to say them but to feel them. So, get yourself into a comfortable position and play some soft relaxing or inspiring music. Do progressive muscle relaxation on yourself (see the following exercise) so you become more receptive to the messages. Repeat the affirmations slowly and allow yourself to move from your head to your heart, allowing yourself to feel the truth of the following affirmation.

 **EXERCISE: PROGRESSIVE MUSCLE RELAXATION TO BUILD CONFIDENCE**

Now that you are comfortable, begin with the top of your head and feel the muscles in your scalp relaxing. Move to your face and feel all the muscles relax, your forehead, your cheeks, your jawline. Move to your neck and feel all the muscles in your neck relax; move to your shoulders, make any little adjustments, and feel your shoulders relax even more now. Feel that relaxation hit your arms and move all the way down and out your fingers. Feel that relaxation move down your neck to your chest, your lungs, your core. As all of your organs relax, feel your back fully relax, feel that relaxation moving down your hips to your legs, down your legs to your ankles, and out your feet. Your whole body is now relaxed.

Now you are ready to repeat and feel the following affirmations:

"What I have to say has value."

"I have a unique perspective."

"I am a leader."

"I am worthy of all my desires."

"I see the magic in others and all around me."

"I allow myself to be in flow."

"I see my heart's desires fulfilled and it feels great."

"Success comes easy to me."

"I am divinely guided."

"I see opportunities."

"I allow greatness to flow through me."

REFLECTIONS:

*Confidence is already within me because I am connected
to the divine intelligence that is all around.
The key is to know my worthiness.*

*Confidence and ego are different. Ego says it is all about me;
confidence says I am capable.*

*Becoming a fearless leader means I am in touch
with who I really am, and I feel good about myself
so I can fearlessly lead others to the greatness
that is within each of them.*

*To fearlessly lead, I need to be brave
about looking at my own triggers
and healing what needs to be healed within first.*

SECTION 2:
AN AWAKENED
LEADER'S
BEST PRACTICES

CHAPTER 10:
THE COST OF BAD LEADERSHIP

I am sure you can recall a time in your own life when you had a horrible boss. You probably dreaded getting up in the morning, hated going to work, and felt more dread than joy about your work hours. It probably leached out into your personal life and made you grumpy. I know I have experienced this and how it made me feel, so it also inspired me to never want someone on my own team to feel this way.

When we want to improve any organization's performance, the first thing to do would be to look at the culture around the leadership team. Leadership plays a pivotal role in the success or failure of any organization. Ineffective or inferior leadership can have far-reaching consequences that extend beyond just the bottom line. It can lead to decreased employee morale, reduced productivity, financial losses, burnout, and an overall unhappy environment.

Let's break down some of these costs, starting with the human side.

THE HUMAN SIDE: COSTS OF INFERIOR LEADERSHIP

1. Employee morale, well-being, and burnout

One of the most significant human costs of inferior leadership is the impact on employee morale and well-being. Employees who are subjected to poor leadership often experience stress, anxiety, and a general sense of dissatisfaction with their jobs. Gallup's "State of the Global Workplace" 2024 report[7] found that only 23 percent of employees worldwide are engaged at work, and ineffective leadership is a primary factor contributing to disengagement.

Inferior leadership can contribute to employee burnout and mental health issues. According to a recent study by the American Psychological Association[8], employees who feel unsupported by their leaders are more likely to report high levels of stress and burnout. The World Health Organization estimates that depression and anxiety disorders cost the global economy over $1 trillion in lost productivity each year.[9]

2. Employee productivity

Inferior leaders can have a detrimental effect on employee productivity. Employees who lack trust and confidence in their leaders are less likely to be motivated to perform at their best. And why should they when it just isn't in their heart to further a goal or vision that they are uncertain about? Trust issues can lead to a sense of being undervalued or underappreciated. When employees perceive that their leaders don't value their contributions or well-being, their motivation can decline because they don't see the point in putting in extra effort.[10]

In essence, trust in leadership provides a foundation of stability and confidence in the workplace. Many of us want to be able to speak with our superiors with candor and openness. When we begin to doubt our leaders, the resulting insecurity, disillusionment, and frustration impact our motivation to perform at our best. Building and maintaining trust between leaders and employees is vital for a healthy and motivating work environment.

ORGANIZATIONAL CULTURE

1. Toxic work culture

Inferior leadership can foster a toxic work culture characterized by fear, distrust, and low morale. Such cultures can have a long-lasting negative impact on an organization, making it difficult to attract and retain top talent. Toxic work cultures can also lead to increased conflict, which can further erode employee morale and productivity.

2. Damage to reputation

A company's reputation is closely tied to the quality of its leadership. Public scandals, ethical lapses, and poor decision-making by leaders can result in significant damage to an organization's reputation. A survey conducted by Edelman[11] found that 46 percent of respondents believed that CEOs are not credible sources of information about their companies, highlighting the erosion of trust in leadership.

FINANCIAL COSTS OF INFERIOR LEADERSHIP

Whenever I go into an organization to do a leadership training or employee wellness program, the first thing I tell leaders is that this will not only help the overall morale of their organization, but a happy team also leads to healthy profits. The opposite is true with ineffective leadership.

1. Decreased profitability

Poor leadership often translates into decreased profitability for organizations and huge financial implications.

"Bad managers cost businesses billions of dollars each year, and having too many of them can bring down a company."[12]

Studies also show that the cost of one poor leader can cost a company more than $126,000 a year due to low productivity and turnover.[13]

Now imagine if you have multiple poor leaders in your organization, it will be detrimental to the success and sustainability of any company, big or small.

I have found this in my own experience, and these studies are proof that if you want to turn any organization around, you need to look at the leadership team and culture first. Many people will look toward the economy or global affairs, and yes, these have a huge impact, but with solid leadership you can ride the storm and come out on top. Leaders who have a strong team can find solutions and learn to pivot when needed. Why are some companies able to persevere through recessions, pandemics, and global uncertainty, while others fail? My belief is that strong leadership that leads to a healthy team-oriented organization is one of the determining factors.

2. Employee turnover

High turnover rates are a significant financial burden on organizations. When employees are dissatisfied with their leaders, they are more likely to leave their jobs in search of better opportunities. A Gallup poll shows that employee turnover / lack of employee retention due to poor leadership practices **costs American companies $1 trillion per year.**[14]

I have always said in my leadership training programs, it is way better to invest in your team, train them, and inspire them then to constantly be replacing them. The cost to replace them is much higher. Now that being said, it does not mean that there are times when an employee is not the right fit. This does happen, but the real cost is when they leave due to not being happy with their boss or the company culture.

3. Decreased engagement

Employee engagement is one of the biggest factors of overall success in any organization. If you have an engaged team, chances are you have a healthy organization. Employee engagement is directly linked to the strength of leadership, which also links to employees' well-being. And the well-being of employees has become one of the key areas of concern when looking at the workforce today.

These statistics[15] on the cost of lack of engagement are staggering:

- Only 34 percent of US employees are engaged at work, while 13 percent are actively disengaged (Gallup).
- Companies with engaged employees outperform those without by up to 202 percent (Gallup).

We are going to explore the importance of engagement later and look at why engagement alone is no longer enough to rely on for the health of your organization.

Inferior leadership exacts a substantial cost on organizations, both financially and in terms of human capital. The statistics presented here underscore the far-reaching consequences of poor leadership on employee engagement, turnover, and organizational culture. It is crucial for organizations to invest in leadership development and foster a culture of effective leadership to mitigate these costs and drive long-term success. By recognizing the impact of inferior leadership and taking steps to address it, organizations can create a healthier and more prosperous future for their employees and stakeholders alike.

Leaders have incredible impact on an organization, either positive or negative. As a leader, your health is directly linked to the health of the company—with health meaning mindset, morale, financial acumen, accountability, and happiness. How you are as an individual directly affects the health of the organization. The best way to create change in your environment is to look in the mirror first.

KEY POINTS:

- The cost of bad leadership of a company is staggering, not only financially but morally as well.

- Leadership style will directly affect the bottom line and culture of any organization.

- Leaders need to look in the mirror and deal with their own anger, frustration, and overwhelm first to positively impact the organization.

CHAPTER 11:
WHAT EMPLOYEES SAY MATTERS MOST

To excel as a leader and be a conscious leader in today's workforce, it is important to look at what employees are saying matters most to them and what they need from their boss. It is easy for a leader to tell you what they think a best practice is, but what employees say should matter more.

Having empathy has become a very important skill as a leader. A mindful leader will step back and take a moment to not take things personally but have empathy for what their team might be going through. It is important to get curious with your team, to ask questions and find ways to connect so you can be the support they need versus a source of stress. As studies have shown, workplace stress and burnout are at an all-time high. As leaders, we need to shift to accommodate and support this. Employees are showing up to work with their own stressors from within and outside work. What employees value more now has shifted over time, and in a post-pandemic world, with an increase in global uncertainty, a stable paycheck is no longer enough to keep an engaged and happy employee. We need to look more at the human side and the interpersonal skills of a leader to give employees what they need most.

WHAT EMPLOYEES VALUE MOST

Well-being. It is no surprise that employees are valuing well-being in the workplace more than ever as we see alarming statistics around burnout and stress. Recent studies[16] have shown 84 percent of employees feel they cannot manage their stress or emotions effectively, and 86 percent of employees believe their organization should prioritize well-being programs. Employees are not just looking for wellness practices such as encouraging breaks, having access to facilities like gyms, or benefits to include wellness activities, but also training and support in wellness such as tangible stress-management tools.

Prioritizing a culture of wellness will have huge payoffs. Leaders who understand this will have a competitive advantage. Statistics show that successful organizations have this in place, which creates a great opportunity for you to get on board with this "new norm."[17]

Effective communication. Employees want to feel safe to speak and to be heard. I know in the emotional healing world I work in, so much of our trauma and lack of self-worth stems from the feeling of not being heard or valued. Studies now show that psychological safety is one of the most important things for strong teams.[18] This means ostentatious listening, so people will feel heard. As a leader, if you can do this, you will make people feel important, valued, and worthy. This is huge!

Flexibility. An important factor for employees to stay in a job or even in considering a new job is the flexibility offered. The pandemic changed the landscape of the corporate world. Employees got a taste of the extra time back in their lives by eliminating commutes. Now it also comes with a cost because it can lead to lack of human connection, which is important for our mental health. A balanced approach might be possible here, but flexibility is not just based on time in the office. It also comes with a level of autonomy for the employee where it is possible to make the hours work for them. It requires a measure on results versus time approach. It allows an employee to book a dentist appointment during the day and make up the work time later. This kind of flexibility goes a long way in the workforce today.

Recognition. Being recognized has always been important to employees, and it always will be because it provides validation. Validation creates and fosters emotional health. As a leader in today's world, when you find different ways to recognize your employees, you are actually creating a more emotionally healthy work environment. The key here is to look for the opportunities, from big to small, and make them part of your intentions for a healthy work environment. We all thrive on validation and kindness. You can show appreciation for loyalty and commitment to bigger company-wide recognition in recognizing the achievement of individual and company-wide key performance indicators (KPIs). There is always an opportunity to show gratitude and appreciation for someone, and this will always be well-received from anyone. A simple thank you can go a long way.

Trust and transparency. Trust is the foundation of any healthy relationship, including the one between employees and leaders. If an employee can trust you, they will be more motivated and feel safer when things are bumpy. One of the ways to increase your employees' trust is through vulnerability, which we will unpack later. But show your human side and own your mistakes rather than trying to cover them up. It is healthy to apologize; this shows inner strength not weakness.

Inclusivity and diversity. In the workplace and everywhere in life, it is important to see every single person as equal and valued regardless of race, gender, sexual orientation, or religious beliefs. We live in a diverse world, thank goodness. This is what makes it interesting. And what employees are asking for and rightly so is for leaders to embrace these differences and allow everyone to feel they belong. Because they do. A 2020 study[19] found that job seekers consider diversity an important factor when evaluating potential employers. This demonstrates that diversity and inclusion are not only moral imperatives but also business necessities.

Opportunities for growth and development. Many employees will be driven by the opportunity for growth. We are all innately driven to evolve and grow, and the workforce creates an opportunity for personal and business development. I have found some of the best leaders are the ones who have grown from within the trenches. In today's competitive job market, employees are looking for opportunities to learn and grow. That previously mentioned study revealed that employees would stay at a company longer if it invested in their career development. This emphasizes the importance of offering training, mentorship, and growth opportunities as a part of effective leadership.

Employees are seeking more than just a paycheck from their leaders; how they feel doing their job has become increasingly important. This is a great thing because it means we need to prioritize the human and emotional needs that have been long neglected. For far too long we have been squashing our emotions as it has not felt safe to be vulnerable at work because of fear of being fired or an underlying policy to just "do your work, then go home." Recognizing the emotional side to employees and tending to these needs makes for a more diverse workforce and allows the emotional healing that is needed. As humans, it has not served us to repress our emotions for decades and generations past. I believe this shows up for us in how we are feeling unhappy or frustrated. We need to be honest with ourselves about our emotions and with our bosses so they can lead with love. This is all good if we pause and listen to what matters most, now and in the future. Leaders who prioritize these values can not only create a more engaged and satisfied workforce but also drive healthier business outcomes. As the workplace continues to evolve, as individuals continue to evolve, leaders who adapt to these changing expectations will be better positioned to lead successful companies in the modern world.

KEY POINTS:

- Going to work for pay is not enough of a motivator to keep and retain healthy, happy employees.

- Emotional safety and healing have become an important part of what is needed in the workplace.

- Psychological safety has become one of the top priorities for employees.

- A culture around well-being in the workplace is no longer a "nice to have" but a necessity.

- It is our innate desire to evolve as humans and this now includes being in touch with our emotions and feeling safe to do so. The workforce needs to create a safe environment and provide the tools to employees to assist and educate with this.

CHAPTER 12:
EMOTIONAL HEALTH FOR SUCCESS

Emotions can scare us, especially the big emotions that we or others can have. However, there is something important to understand as a heart-centered leader: Emotions are part of life and part of everyone on the planet. Many of the tensions and conflicts that we face in life are mostly from either repressed emotions, emotional baggage that we carry, or ignoring and suppressing our emotions over time, which then build up. As an emotional healer, I have learned with my own life and those of my clients that true liberation comes if we are brave enough to look at our emotions and heal them. When we suppress them, they tend to build, what we call in hypnosis, a pressure cooker in the body until the lid pops. When we experience those uncomfortable conflicts, it is usually someone's buildup of unhealed emotions and beliefs that have now popped up and it comes out as either anger or sadness, or shame or guilt—the lower frequencies.

I can understand that for most people these types of conflicts or situations make us uncomfortable, so we might try and avoid them at all costs by either ignoring the situation or brushing it away. The problem is it will never go away. It will rear its ugly head later, and maybe with a different face, but the issue will always follow you.

One of the most powerful things we can do is to face our emotions so we can transcend the issue rather than let it persist. As a leader, this is one of the healthiest things you can do, not only in your own life when your emotions are raging, but also when you see it happening with team members. Face the problem or emotion that has been raised so it can be healed. However, the traditional workplace has never been a safe space for emotions. Previous generations of leadership didn't make it a safe place for feelings; it was more the motto to "suck it up and get it done." Leaders from the baby boomer generation were not trained to lean into emotions and ask how you were feeling. This would have been a foreign and very awkward concept. I believe it still is today, but it is what we need as a society. We need to heal emotionally, and we can only do this by facing the feelings.

A recent study from the Workforce Institute[20] found that managers have just as much of an impact on people's mental health as their spouse (both 69 percent) and even more of an impact than their doctor (51 percent) or therapist (41 percent). These findings are very telling, and as leaders, we can look at this and take away that we create impact. So, ask yourself what kind of impact do you want to create—positive or negative?

First, it is important to note that you have a huge impact on your team's well-being, which is a huge responsibility and something that should be prioritized, especially when that study also found that 56 percent of Gen X, 69 percent of Millennials, and up to 70 percent of Gen Z would most likely trade in a high-paying job for mental health support instead. Times have changed, and you can no longer ignore the incredible impact you have on your team's well-being. Employees are prioritizing mental health support more now than in the history of the workforce because it is what's needed.

Second, when you choose to become a heart-centered leader you will see the huge opportunity you have to create a healthy team because you will understand the importance of leaning into emotions and not shying away from them. You will understand that to create a work culture around psychological safety, you must get comfortable with emotions. I could tell right away when an employee was off. You can feel their energy when you open up to it. I used to think it would be easier to ignore, but I knew that was not proactive and could lead to bigger issues. So, I would always take the employee to the side and do a check-in, ask how they were or if they needed extra support today. Many times, they would look at me in awe and ask how I knew. I would reply by saying I could feel their energy and that they seemed different that day. The end result was they always felt cared for. They knew I was busy, but not too busy to do an emotional check-in.

To further understand your opportunity as a leader to create a safe, healthy culture, it is important to understand the three basic human emotional needs that we all have. Every human on the planet has these three needs, and when one feels threatened, we usually get a kink in our emotional field that will come out sideways.

The three emotional needs we all have are:

1. Love
2. Safety
3. Belonging

As a leader, if you can understand that this is what everyone needs to feel whole, then you can begin to foster an environment where everyone can feel love, safety, and a sense of belonging. If we spend some time in our daily routines to encourage this, the payoff will be far greater than if we just focus on company logistics. The human side in leadership has become top priority, and if we dare to lean in and learn here, we will see great opportunity.

HOW TO CREATE A CULTURE AROUND LOVE, SAFETY, AND BELONGING:

The key part is recognizing the importance and not denying it. Once you do, it just becomes a way of doing business rather than something that needs to be added to your plate.

The first emotional need for every employee is love, which is caring for an individual; it is making them feel seen and heard. This is one of the most empowering things you can do for anyone—imagine a team member feeling that at work. You will create ripples of impact as they will emulate this behavior, and so on. Love can become part of your language and how you see the individuals on your team. Ask yourself a simple question to become aligned with love:

Is the way I am asking or telling someone to do something coming from a loving energy or place within?

Check in with your tone of voice and your body language; it will tell you a lot. And check in with your own emotions when you are engaging with someone else. Are you frustrated or in a loving state? This is how you show up and cultivate a loving environment. The loving and caring part must come from within. You as the leader set the tone. Now, please don't mistake this for never being clear or setting expectations or, when needed, taking disciplinary action. Of course, you need to, but it is the way we do things that will make a difference to how it lands or is received. Love can always be the frequency, even in conflict resolution. You will find that the more you lead with love, the less conflict there will ultimately be. If you raise the environment to the frequency of love, some of your team (the toxic ones) may fall away. That is okay. You will attract others who will fit the love vibe.

The second emotional need is safety. It is important for your team to feel safe to express themselves, to not feel like they might lose their jobs or be judged if they share their experiences or views. It is important, as a leader, to ask them what they think often, get their opinions, and make them part of the solutions. Safety means that you allow each team member to share and not just a select few. You value everyone's opinions and see each team member as an essential part of your organization.

Which connects to the third emotional need, belonging. Each individual needs to feel they are important and belong to a greater collective. One way to help a team member feel that sense of belonging is by connecting the company mission and purpose back to them as an individual. To allow them to be empowered to move the company closer to their goals. To give positive feedback and encouragement and allow them to feel appreciated because you recognize their contribution. The best way to do this is not being predictable about it in yearly reviews or bonuses but looking for the small daily or weekly opportunities of gratitude toward the employee's contribution. This will create huge ripples of impact; it will foster a healthy emotional environment that feels so wonderful to be a part of. Any leader can do this when they utilize their tuning forks to see the opportunities to lead with their heart. Your employees will want to work for you, they will want to do better, they will want to continually grow and evolve. It is a beautiful thing!

LEADERSHIP EMOTIONAL CHECKLIST:

✓ Have emotional check-ins. How are you feeling about your job? What do you enjoy the most? What do you enjoy the least?

✓ Look for social clues. You will always be able to tell if someone is off or having a bad day because you can feel their energy, see their body language. Check in and ask if there is anything you can do for them.

✓ Have team meetings. Make sure there is opportunity for everyone's input. Look out for the quiet ones and encourage feedback and engagement. Conversational turn-taking is an important piece of psychological safety.

✓ Have fun. Create opportunities to lighten the load and bring laughter into the office or workplace.

✓ Share helpful tools. Give your team tools to manage and regulate emotions, especially stress. Breathing techniques, meditations, tapping, outdoor breaks, etc., help immensely.

✓ Encourage wellness, always. Be the leader.

So, dial in to their emotions rather than run away from them. You will be missing huge opportunities for greatness otherwise.

KEY POINTS:

- Tune in to and prioritize your employees' emotional needs.

- Create a culture around love, safety, and belonging. This will meet the three emotional needs that we all have as humans, and it will create loyalty and a healthy corporate culture.

- Face emotions rather than fear them. Avoiding them always builds bigger conflict. Facing them means you can help your team to shift with ease.

CHAPTER 13:
KINDNESS WILL TAKE YOU FAR

Kindness. Such a simple concept yet so powerful when it comes to creating meaningful and impactful results as a leader.

Two simple words: BE KIND.

That is it. If there is anything you take from this book, let it be the lessons from this chapter on kindness. Kindness will get you so much further than hate, anger, frustration, pride, or jealousy.

Kindness is not only a love language but a human language. As humans, we respond to kindness in a positive way, and we create ripples of beauty and positivity through kindness. We are meant to be kind because it feels better to give and receive kindness.

When you are in a difficult situation that you want to shift, sprinkling it with kindness is one of the most powerful ways to create change, rather than leaning into anger and frustration, which will grow the problem. Your words have the power to heal and uplift or create emotional wounds and spread negativity. Your words can change a person's life for the better when you speak with kindness. This is not only true in the leadership space but also in any relationship you have in your life. Kindness will always feel better, both to the receiver and the giver. Think about how you feel when you are kind versus when you are angry.

If this is the case, why do we not see more kindness in the work-place, especially coming from our leaders? Because this comes from emotional health that must start from within. You need to be happy within yourself to be kind to others and to see the opportunities for kindness. One of my favorite sayings is "You will catch more flies with honey than with vinegar." Thus, you will get more of what you want with sweetness and more of what you don't want with bitterness.

Part of the problem as to why we struggle with kindness is we learn from a young age that "nice people come in last." We have these messages drilled into our heads, we internalize them, and they become the truth. We have also heard messages that you need to be tough to get ahead. Sometimes, toughness is confused as needing to be mean. We have learned to criticize ourselves and others from a young age. I always go back to this connection to our self-worth. I also see with many leaders that they feel they won't be respected if they are not tough. They worry their team will walk all over them. Meaning they will have no control. This old-school style of leadership has no room in our current workplace.

One of the first things I noticed when I went back to run our family business is that many of the managers were in fear. They were afraid to speak out, they were afraid of the dismal numbers in our financial meetings, they were afraid of ultimately losing their jobs. This style of management was not working because it was creating a negative cycle of fear and bad results. Long after the 2008 recession, our business did not recover because the management style needed to change. I am not knocking the way the generation did it before me. It worked then, which is the way many people of the baby boomer generation handled things. Kindness was not their language; toughness got results. Kindness was viewed as weak. The truth is, kindness is a strength. And I can honestly say that this was a big reason our business experienced ten-year growth year after year until we sold it. It was through kindness. It was through seeing that each person played a very important role. No matter if you were a housekeeper or a senior manager, you were important. It was through acknowledging everyone, connecting, learning more about them and what was important. It was through love-based inspiration versus fear based. It was through seeing what people were capable of rather than seeing their downfalls. Kindness is seeing greatness in people. It's allowing others to shine. Kindness shows through compliments versus criticism.

KINDNESS DOES NOT MEAN NO STRUCTURE

I don't want to confuse kindness with butterflies and roses all day every day. There will be hard moments and tough decisions you need to make. There will be times when you need to fire people because it is the best for the organization and ultimately for them. But how you approach these situations will make all the difference. If it is through kindness, even the tough conversations can be easier. You still need to have clarity in the job, the expectations, clear KPIs, direction, and goals. All of this is necessary for an inspired team. But you can do all of that through the lens of kindness and create much further-reaching ripples of productivity, performance, happiness, and organizational health.

Step way back and ask yourself: Why do I do what I do? Is it for the money? Is it for the glory? Is it because I feel stuck and don't have a choice? Is it for purpose? Whatever your answer, hopefully you do what you do for the joy of it. That is what the whole purpose of this life is. For joy. And through kindness we can experience more of that joy. Kindness means you as a leader see your team member as a unique individual. Kindness means you care. WE need that currency today. WE need to heal our organizations to create greatness, and through kindness, we can create a more engaged and happier team. You will become a magnet through kindness rather than a repellent through the lower emotions of fear and anger or worse, indifference.

ACTIVATING KINDNESS WITHIN

We all can and need to activate more kindness within. You can bring this to your homes and teams. All the people around you will benefit from this. Sometimes it is with the people closest to us where we can begin to practice the kindness muscle the most. I know I am always telling my kids to be kind to each other. They are teenagers, and wow, it seems much easier for them to criticize rather than be nice. I often bring it back to asking how that makes them feel. Then we get into the game of verbal ping-pong where one will say, "Yeah, well, he said it first—" and it escalates. This happens at work as well. "He was such a jerk, so I am going to . . ." (fill in the blanks). We often play ping-pong, exchanging harsh comments back and forth. It never ends well and it always feels shitty. The power you have is to activate more kindness within, so let's go on a little healing journey to do this. In Chapter 3 you learned about tapping, which is an effective tool we can use to shift any emotions we are feeling that don't serve. It is a great way to diffuse anger or heal your anger triggers and feel more kindness in your heart. It is normal to feel anger; it's only human—the real success is to feel it and shift it. Follow along whenever you feel the trigger of frustration or anger.

EXERCISE: TAPPING SEQUENCE FOR KINDNESS

REPEAT:

- **Karate chop:** Even though I feel this anger and frustration and I don't like the way it makes me feel, I deeply love and accept myself anyway.

- **Karate chop:** Even though I don't like how this anger makes me feel, but (they) frustrate me so much, I deeply love and forgive myself.

- **Eyebrow:** This anger.

- **Side of the eye:** This frustration, I get so triggered and annoyed.

- **Under the eye:** I want to yell and scream even though I know that will make it worse.

- **Under the nose:** I don't want to be mean; this is not who I am.

- **Chin:** I just wish they wouldn't trigger me so much.

- **Under the collarbone or sore spot:** I know the trigger and the anger is mine; it is for me to shift.

- **Under arm:** I am a kind person, even though that is not how I have acted.

- **Top of the head:** I am choosing to lead with more kindness; it feels so much better.

REPEAT THE SEQUENCE FROM THE EYEBROW TO LET GO OF THE ANGER:

"I am letting it go."

"I am letting all this anger go."

"I am letting go of all the emotional roots of this anger and frustration."

"I am giving myself permission to let it go."

"Letting it all go now."

"Letting it go now."

"I am choosing to let it all go now."

"I can and will let it all go now."

REPEAT THE SEQUENCE FROM THE EYEBROW TO ANCHOR IN KINDNESS:

"I am choosing kindness."

"I am activating more kindness in my body."

"Kindness feels so much better."

"I am a kind person."

"I love myself deeply and forgive myself."

"I am choosing kindness."

"I know kindness will go a long way."

"I know I will get a more desired outcome through kindness."

The more we tap on kindness, the more we can activate it as our go-to frequency. It is so important to own the anger and frustration first, not to deny it, and to forgive yourself for it. You are human and you will have these emotions. Many of them come to us as a signal of our own healing that is needed. When you feel your body acting from a place of kindness more often, then you will know you have shifted, and you can watch the magic unfold around you because it will. And trust me, as a kind leader, I get much better results from my team. It is the only way forward.

KEY POINTS:

- Kindness is one of your most powerful tools.

- Words spoken with kindness can positively change someone's life.

- You need to first feel and cultivate kindness within by healing your own anger and frustration. You are a powerful healer and can do this.

- As a leader, being kind does not make you weak but shows strength.

- Kindness and clarity around job expectations can and need to coexist.

CHAPTER 14:
THE POWER IN PRESENCE

One of the greatest illusions we have as leaders and high achievers is the feeling of the need to multitask. Get as much done as possible as fast as you can because this means you are more productive, right? This means you have accomplished more, doesn't it? I used to really believe this and felt it was the only way to be successful. In fact, when I interviewed people in my first role as a manager, I would ask multitasking questions during the interview. If you answered these with enthusiasm and could give me examples, you would have a gold star beside your name. Ugh, if I could go back to my younger self, I would say, "Stop the bullshit. You are kidding yourself if you think multitasking is something to be proud of or even possible."

Multitasking is a flawed concept of the past. You cannot do it. It is an illusion; you can only do one thing at once. When you think you are doing multiple things at once you are simply fracturing your energy and not doing either task well. You are dividing yourself into fragments, and the people around you are getting that fragmented version of you. This leads to burnout and a feeling of overwhelm because you are running a mile a minute and not replenishing your energy throughout the day. Think about it for a second. Can you be present with someone in a conversation while responding to an email? Impossible. Your energy is split, so someone is getting the distracted version of you. I used to pride myself all the time on my ability to multitask until I realized I hated the way it made me feel and my team got the sense that I was "too busy" to have focused or undistracted conversations. This will never leave the person feeling good because they never get the sense that they are important enough to have your undivided attention.

A recent Google study[21] looked at what the most important thing was in building a strong team in the workplace. They found that psychological safety was the most important thing. Psychological safety consists of two things: ostentatious listening and equality in conversational turn-taking. It is impossible to create an environment of ostentatious listening when you are multitasking. To be an ostentatious listener you must be able to make eye contact, paraphrase, and create engagement. These are really important things for a team member to feel psychologically safe, which has become one of the key factors in distinguishing between highly successful teams. So, it has never been more important to hit pause, do one thing at a time, and do it well.

I get into this argument with my husband all the time to stop multitasking and be an active listener. It is an old program we have in our heads, and it is outdated. The feeling of "I won't have enough time if I am not doing multiple things at once." This is an awful way to live because we can never feel the magic of the present if we're constantly distracted. Have you ever had a conversation with your partner and then two days later they have no recollection of that talk? You probably felt dismissed or not important or heard. Not feeling heard creates a huge emotional void in us, and hence, as a leader, one of the healthiest things you can do for your employees is to listen! This is why ostentatious listening has become such an important practice for highly conscious leaders.

We have an even bigger challenge when we are parental leaders and leaders in schools as our kids are so distracted and addicted to their phones. It has become harder to have engaging conversations with teenagers as they have their heads buried in their devices. As leaders, however, when we want to see change, we must model this first. I can't blame my teenagers for being on their phone if I am as well. So, it is better to tell someone, "I can't give you my full attention right now, I am in the middle of this; please give me five minutes" rather than continue in a half-listening mode, not really being present.

I often tell my team I am closing my door to do uninterrupted and focused work. They have learned to respect that because I also give them my full attention when we are in strategy or marketing and planning meetings, or if we are simply having bonding and rapport conversations. No matter what you are doing, if you can give the person your presence, you are giving the best gift. You show them you care and they are valued. This is not only great leadership practice but also great practice as a great partner, friend, parent, and colleague. You will never go wrong when you choose to be present with someone because it fosters deeper connection, and we need connection. We are starving for it. Real connection with one human to another, not connection on social media based on likes or followers, which is not real connection.

Focused work is the most effective, and sometimes you need to close your door, tune out the outside world, and get it done. My office door is closed right now as I am writing this book. My phone is on "do not disturb," and 100 percent of my focus is on writing.

This is how we get things done in a productive and efficient way. I could never finish this book and run a business and household if I did not block time off for focused work. However, when I am collaborating with my team, I am focused on that and not my phone. Focused work or being present with the task at hand is the best way to increase your productivity, which really means efficient output. This is my motto: Work smarter not harder. And the way to do this is focus and be present on the task you're doing.

Let the magic of being present show up in all areas of your life. Give yourself permission in whatever you are doing to be present, whether that is walking, exercising, cooking, going out with friends, working, you name it, you will get more out of life by being present wherever you are. I also know how important it is to set yourself up for the most productive workday by pacing yourself right. That means don't book back-to-back meetings in your day. Take breaks in between. Book time in your calendar for your loved ones or have what I call "sacred time" in the day, meaning time to be present. Create a work culture around psychological safety where you become an ostentatious listener. You will not only see the difference around you in how people respond to you, but you will also realize you are filling your emotional cup and becoming way more productive.

KEY POINTS:

- Psychological safety is one of the key metrics in building a successful team.

- You can only do this by being present and an active listener.

- Productivity goes up when you are focused.

- You will have more energy in your day by avoiding the illusion of multitasking.

- You will see the magic around you by being more present with yourself, your tasks, and others in your life.

CHAPTER 15:
GIVE YOUR TEAM THE TOOLS
TO SUCCEED

There are times when you will be challenged as a leader and in life, and it is during these times that your strengths will need to be put into action. And there is a balanced approach to creating an independent and empowered team and a dependent team. You want them to swim on their own, but you also want to give them the tools and help if they are sinking. Are you willing to get into the trenches with your team? Do they know you will have their back? Do you support them in the tough times?

All these things matter when building and creating a strong team and becoming a heart-centered leader. The strength of a team and a leader will always be tested during the hard times. It is during these times that you will know what you are made of and what you are capable of. Setting an intention and mindset around team support will be one of the most important things you do as a leader. We know that burnout is higher than it has ever been in the workforce. People are suffering with their mental health, and the important thing is having the right tools in the tool kit when things get tough. A strong leader can help their team get through the tough times, can smooth out some of the bumps, and can make even the impossible seem possible.

When the chips are down there are two key things a leader can do that will help their team have the mental capacity to get through:

1. Tell them you believe in them. Tell them they will get through this. Break down the big problem into pieces and focus on the things that they can manage and that are in their control.

2. Be willing to get into the trenches with them. Support them, take on some of the load if necessary, or at least show up and be by their side if possible. This will also build respect and give them the confidence that they have your support.

When I was running our business of over 350 employees in twelve different departments with more than fifty staff in leadership positions, there were many moving parts. Our philosophy was a hands-on approach from top down. As owners, we believed in doing whatever it took to support our teams with a balance of empowerment. This meant if we were short-staffed, we rolled up our sleeves, served tables, and did what it took. Do I believe this builds respect for your team? Yes. Do you need to be careful that this creates an unhealthy dependency? Also, yes. Now, as an owner or manager, you also need to be careful because if you are too hands-on it will be very difficult to scale or grow your business. If you feel you must do everything yourself or that everything needs your approval and you don't have systems in place, you will become burned out. Trust me, I learned the hard way when first getting into leadership. I thought I had to be there seven days a week, which led to burnout. But even worse, my team became too dependent on me and could not make decisions or put out fires on their own. So, to be clear, the key here is a balanced approach. If you find yourself in the trenches all the time with your team, there is something wrong. The key is a willingness to get in the trenches in the rare case the team needs your help.

Over the years coaching and consulting with many leaders and business owners, I always noticed that the most successful teams that had harmony and a healthy outlook were the ones where the leaders had the balanced approach of empowerment and support. Sometimes this is putting the foot on the gas and then the brake. Giving your team the wings to fly but having a net to help if they crash. It is believing in their talents and rolling up your sleeves when needed.

From a team member perspective, the best kind of bosses are the ones who give their team the space to do their jobs, without micromanaging. But who also ensure their team members can count on them for help when needed. It is the same with our kids. We want to raise them with independence and allow them to figure things out while giving them support and guidance. It is not up to us to solve all their problems but guide them to find the solutions.

As leaders, the best way to find this balance is to tap in to your intuitive center and ask yourself for the answers. How would I want to feel supported in this situation? If I was my own boss, what would be the most important thing right now? Remember that we are all human and might not always have the answers, so when you sense or see a team member struggling, you can always ask, "What is the best way I can support you right now?" You will know they feel safe if they ask for help. This will mean they are comfortable with you as a leader and don't feel they are inadequate. That is the balance as a leader. Never make someone feel inadequate because they might need help. This is the beautiful relationship of give and take, help and support.

When times are tough, one of the most important things you can rely on is having tools in your own tool management kit and also ones you can share with your team. Managing stress is the key to not only living a healthy lifestyle but also allowing us grace through the tougher times.

EXERCISE: STRESS-MANAGEMENT TOOL KIT REFERENCE LIST

Make a list of the things you do to help balance yourself when stressed, then refer to this when needed. In your next team meeting, do a group share around stress-management tools. Your team will inspire each other and learn some best practices here.

My stress-management tool kit:

KEY POINTS:

- Be willing to roll up your sleeves and get in the trenches.

- When in doubt, ask, "What is the best way I can support you?"

- Never make anyone feel inadequate. Explain that it is normal to need support—we all do—and that is your job as their leader to be there for them.

- Do regular check-ins!

- Grow your stress management tool kit as a team.

CHAPTER 16:
WORK SMARTER, NOT HARDER

If you are like me, most of your life conditioning has been around working hard to get ahead. This belief system was so entrenched in me that for many years my success as a leader meant that I had to constantly prove myself by working the hardest and the longest. I'd sometimes work a ridiculous number of hours a week, so all that was left was my head hitting the pillow for a few hours to wake and repeat the insanity all over again. Working seventy- to eighty-hour workweeks is not sustainable and will throw you out of balance with your mental and physical health. We are not robots, meaning we need nourishment. We are also multidimensional beings, meaning we are not meant to put it in overdrive for long periods of time solely being focused on one thing, as it will put the other areas of life out of balance and leave us feeling depleted. There are times in life when we are working on a deadline or a major project that will require long hours and there is nothing wrong with that when it is short term. In fact, it can feel fun and exhilarating and create a huge sense of accomplishment when working to get something over the finish line.

The destructive belief is when we feel the only way to work is by working at an inhuman pace, when working long hours around the clock becomes a normal state of mentality. Even worse is when we connect how hard we work to our sense of worth as a human and as a leader. This is when many people feel "out of balance" because our true nature is not to sacrifice many things that matter for success, or to focus on career at the cost of health or relationships. Our true nature is always harmony.

The key to "balance," or working smarter, always comes down to your belief in self. I have talked to many successful leaders who try so hard to convince me that it is the industry they are in or the environment they work in or the type of work they do that justifies the crazy hours and the lack of balance in their lives. But the truth is, it comes down to what you believe in. I have witnessed many of these leaders changing industries completely, and the same habits follow them. Because you take you everywhere you go, and until you change, your environment cannot change.

Many clients I work with suffer from anxiety. They often tell me they just have to get through this next project, or they need to hire someone else so they will be able to work fewer hours. I often ask them when the last time was when they felt they had work-life balance. Many of them draw a blank because they can't remember. Their belief that they need to work longer and harder at all costs has become a core belief. And this belief dictates their workaholic mentality. We all have the same twenty-four hours in a day, no exceptions, and so the only thing that is different between the burned-out employee and the one who is happy is how they are managing their time.

Time management is connected to productivity, and it has been proven that stress decreases productivity. If you are not blocking some time for self-care to manage your stress, then you are unable to be as efficient as others who do. This goes back to the notion of upgrading your belief that "I am a priority." Once you believe this, you will find the time to nourish, replenish, and therefore increase your output at work.

For many years, I worked in hospitality. When running a hotel, the operation was 365 days a year, twenty-four hours a day. We see a lot of burnout with leaders in this industry, and I was one. But I knew I could not change the industry; it was what it was. The only thing I could change was how I approached it, how I had to heal my sense of self-worth regardless of how many hours I worked, how I had to set up systems and empower my team, and how I ultimately had to realign with my values to live my best life while being successful. One of the best ways to manage your time more effectively is to realign with your values. What is the most important thing to you?

What I will tell you is all this is possible when you change you, when you upgrade the internal belief system that has you convinced that the only way is to work out of balance. As a leader, if you find yourself hoping or praying for things to get smoother or to calm down in your external environment, you will be waiting your lifetime. And this is why many people feel they are living their lives on repeat and can't stop until their body speaks louder.

KEY PRINCIPLES FOR TIME MANAGEMENT:
- Respect yourself first.
- Block schedule things that are a priority (your breaks, exercise, focused creative time, admin time, employee time, etc.).
- Do a personal value exercise and align it with time.
- Delegate, empower, communicate.
- Set boundaries with colleagues, clients, and your team. (2 a.m. emails are a no-go!)

- Teach your team balance by doing it yourself.
- Have focused time with no distractions. (Put your phone on do not disturb when you need to get stuff done. The stop and start and the distractions will fracture your focus and decrease your efficiency.)
- Get your team to do the personal value exercise.

 **EXERCISE: PERSONAL VALUE**

What I value the most:

Where I spend most of my time:

What needs more nourishment (time):

Let this exercise bring awareness to what needs more nourishment. What parts of your life are being neglected so you can nourish them? When we nourish all the parts of us, we are in better flow, and we get more done in less time because we feel good.

KEY POINTS:

- We all have twenty-four hours in a day; it is all in what you prioritize.

- Working smarter means being more efficient and productive.

- Productivity goes up when stress goes down.

- Focused time with no distractions allows efficiency to go up.

- Block schedule the things that matter the most.

CHAPTER 17:
COMMUNICATION EXCELLENCE
FOR TODAY'S WORKFORCE

Communication is the glue that holds any relationship together. Most breakdowns of relationships seem to be connected to a breakdown of communication. To a missing of each other, of not feeling heard, not feeling understood, and not feeling like you matter. And most importantly, breakdowns often result when someone does not even feel safe to communicate their truth or feelings.

When communication flows, with openness and honesty and a level of safe vulnerability, the relationship can flourish, despite differences. In fact, differences are necessary and will always be there. It is healthy to have a difference of opinion. How can we all think alike all the time? First, that would be incredibly boring and impossible, but also to have a strong healthy team, you need differences—you want different opinions and perspectives. This is how we grow, evolve, and expand. These are all good things if the communication with you and your team is healthy. If communication is unhealthy, it starts to build debris and residue, and over time this creates stress, blocks, and a lot of disharmonies among the team. So, in order to have a healthy team, you need to have healthy communication.

Spending years consulting other leaders and owners to grow their business, I noted that the ones who struggled the most were the ones who operated in silos versus a team. Working as a team means you need to communicate. And healthy communication means setting a tone around speaking openly and giving constructive feedback with a balance of phrasing success. It is about creating a safe environment where team members can share their ideas and be part of the big picture but also putting systems in place to ensure healthy communication. Whether you are running a large or small operation, the tone around healthy communication needs to be set by you, the leader. The more open you are as a leader, the more open they will feel they can be. The more real you are as a leader, the more real they will feel they can be.

Let's break down some simple strategies and processes to implement in your organization to ensure effective communication.

YEARLY REVIEWS

In one of my first roles as a leader, I underestimated the importance of having yearly or biannual reviews with my employees. I was more focused on hitting my business goals than I was on the personnel. The business was booming in year one, we were hitting all our targets, and most importantly, we had a healthy vibe among the team. Well, at least in the beginning, while everything was still new and exciting. But after a while, the luster of a new business wears off and your cracks start showing. I noticed staff cutting corners, and there was some conflict and overall business troubles, mostly to do with running the team. I was taking the team for granted. I didn't make the time to sit with them one-on-one, to make them feel important and go over individual goals. This time not only showed everyone I cared but also helped hold them—and me—accountable.

Now in my own business, and over the years as a consultant, I have always prioritized the implementation of evaluations. And what has amazed me over the years has been that I always notice a difference in morale in an organization that has a standard operating procedure (SOP) in place for evaluations and those that do not. Having an SOP is a game changer for staff morale and overall long-term performance. At a minimum, yearly reviews work well; in some organizations, if you can do a six-month review, then great. The key is to commit and deliver on time.

SOME KEY THINGS FOR SUCCESSFUL AND EFFECTIVE REVIEWS:

- Have a SOP about reviews in your organization. Each leader should do one for their direct reports and include:
  - Frequency/schedule of the reviews.
  - A standard template or structure for your leaders to follow.
- Your reviews need to be two-way, meaning a space for employees to openly share their feedback. Ask specific questions.
- No distractions. This time is for them, so clear your schedule for focused time on the individual without interruptions or distractions.
- Have a balance of celebrating success and areas of improvement.
- You can get them to fill out a copy of their review for themselves and compare your score and areas to improve. This is a great way for them to self-reflect.
- Include KPIs and goals as specific ways you can measure their success. This will vary from industry to industry.
- If possible, build a monetary bonus into the KPIs.
- Include completion of reviews as a KPI for your leadership team. This ensures reviews are done as a company standard.

FREQUENT TEAM MEETINGS, INCLUDING OFF-SITES

No matter the size of your organization or which industry you are in, having team meetings is imperative. In the following chapter, we will discuss how to create impactful team meetings. The important thing here is to have structured meeting times. This might include a monthly meeting with your senior leadership team. It might include a daily meeting with your team to go over the day's tasks. Generally, a formal meeting is scheduled and can be expected, and an informal meeting is something more impromptu to discuss things on the fly. If these are not things you have in place, you can start quarterly and build it up to monthly or weekly meetings. The key is that team meetings are a great avenue to build healthy communication. It is also great for team building and morale when done right, which we will discuss in the next chapter.

Take your team off-site. I am asked to speak at a lot of off-site meetings and conferences for teams and leaders. Every time, I notice that people seem more relaxed, more open, more talkative. They let their guard down. There is a huge benefit to taking your team off-site for a team meeting or team building. Not only does this facilitate bonding and rapport, but it's also a great chance to have effective, connected communication. It's a great time to talk about the future vision and set goals, as well as reflect on past success and to celebrate. It allows for more personal conversations, getting to know your team more intimately and what is important to them, such as family and hobbies. In today's world, this is so important. Off-site meetings also take you away from the daily operational distractions and allow for focused and productive time. They are even more important if your company is remote. This gives you a chance to connect in person, and communication face-to-face will always be different to that over a screen.

OPEN-AND CLOSED-DOOR POLICY—A BALANCE OF THE TWO

I used to believe in an open-door policy when I first started in leadership. I thought this was great and meant my staff would always feel comfortable talking, and I wanted to be approachable to ensure healthy communication. In truth, it got out of hand. I was constantly interrupted throughout the day, sometimes for the stupidest and littlest things. I was creating an environment where I was always available. They didn't have to think because I was always there with the answer for them. I created an environment of complete dependence on me. Yikes. This created great stress and often my whole day was answering questions, which meant my evenings were spent getting my work done. I was working around the clock with no balance in my life.

Now I do an open- and closed-door policy. When my door is open, it means "please knock and come in"; if it is closed, it means "do not bug me, I'm busy." I think it is so important to set this culture and environment for your team and to have boundaries, for many reasons. One, there are times when it is not possible to be available. As the boss or leader, there are many things that need your attention during the day and sometimes that is uninterrupted time. If you are in a meeting, you need to not be interrupted; if you are doing someone's evaluation, you need your door closed. The list goes on. There will be times when your door needs to be closed to be productive.

On the other hand, open your door as often as you can. It does create an environment of inclusivity, trust, and openness. It is in the balance where you will thrive, as you will be more productive but also available for your team, which is essential as a leader.

Right now, as I am writing this chapter, my door is closed. I always tell my assistant when I need focused, uninterrupted time, then I close my door. It is an open communication relationship with my door closed at times. Set the expectations and the culture, but have a balance because productivity is key.

TEAM HUDDLES AND COFFEE CHATS

Impromptu team huddles and coffee chats are a great way to connect and keep the channels of communication healthy with your team members. This is effective whether you're remote or in person. When your team is at the office, these can be easier to facilitate and be spontaneous. If you are a remote or mostly remote team, you may want to have scheduled team huddles and coffee chats.

TUNE IN—THE UNSPOKEN WORDS

A lot of healthy communication is being able to tune in and be aware of the energy of your team. This communication skill of the conscious leader is sensing the unspoken words and things that might be bugging them that they are not verbalizing. Our body language and thoughts also carry energy, which means someone doesn't even need to open their mouth for you to be able to feel the mood they are in. Pay attention to the next person who walks into the room and tune in to their energy. At times, it might be wise to just do an impromptu check-in to maintain a healthy environment and not let toxic energy build up.

KEY POINTS:

- Any healthy relationship is based on healthy communication, where the individual can be real, vulnerable, and safe to share their thoughts.

- Studies show poor communication from leaders is one of the major causes of workplace stress.

- Simple standard procedures to have in place to ensure consistent communication from all your leaders and to create a healthy culture around communication are the following:
    - Yearly/biannual evaluations
    - Structured weekly/monthly meetings
    - Team huddles / coffee chat check-ins
    - Off-site meetings or team building
    - Open- and closed-door policy
    - The unspoken words

CHAPTER 18:
ENGAGING MEETINGS ARE A MUST

From the time I began my leadership journey, I knew the importance of holding engaging meetings and would use the time as an opportunity to create comradery and build the team's energy. Attendance and feedback were always good as the team would be pumped afterward, engaged, and excited for the workday or month ahead. Sometimes for longer meetings, I would bring in a speaker or have a personal touch of some sort. I would always make them fun and interesting and never the same.

In my consulting days, when conducting team meetings, I learned a lot from others—especially regarding how not to do things. During infrequent meetings held by leaders who would procrastinate, discontent was so prevalent that employees would often use the meetings as a platform for voicing complaints. I saw leaders use meetings to criticize or sabotage a team's performance by sowing doubt in the minds of their employees. I saw leaders trying to motivate through fear, and team morale would take a nosedive. No one would speak up because they were too afraid. In these cases, people dreaded the monthly meeting. A meeting should be productive and worthwhile, as our time is sacred. The power of these meetings can make or break your company culture.

As discussed in the previous chapter, holding meetings is essential to creating a culture around healthy communication. As a leader, you have a lot of power to create positive impact through meetings if done right.

Some of the pitfalls leaders make when conducting meetings:

1. They are inconsistent with meetings and timing.
2. They often cancel or reschedule meetings.
3. They are not prepared with an agenda.
4. They do not have structure.
5. They do not have a scheduled end time.
6. They are boring.
7. They lack balanced interaction, as a few people monopolize the conversation.

Having team meetings can be an excellent way to create connections, communicate objectives and feedback, and create a motivating environment. However, if you fall into any of these listed traps, then these meetings can be causing more harm than good.

The key to creating impact and success is not just to hold a meeting but to hold an engaging meeting. How do you do this?

FOLLOW THE FIVE P'S TO CREATE AN ENGAGING MEETING:

- Passionate
- Purposeful
- Prompt
- Present
- Personal

Passion. When you are passionate about meetings, you are more engaged, and your team will feel that passion. Many times, it is more in how you say something then what you say. So, don't be dull and boring. Remember, as a leader, the importance of starting your day right by taking care of you first, so you have the energy you need to create impact. Another way to invoke your passion is by reminding yourself of why you do what you do, and remembering the influence you have over others. Your impact will be directly affected by the level of passion you bring. The opposite of passion is dull, and if you show up dull, your meetings will be dull and disengaged.

Purposeful. It's simple; make every meeting have a purpose. Tell your team the purpose of the meeting and outline the agenda with the goal right at the beginning. It is always good to state the purpose in the beginning so everyone can better engage and understand the intent. Use a powerful statement like "It is essential for us to have this meeting so we can all be on the same page and aligned on this . . ." This will set the stage and allow them to understand the importance. Do not leave it up to guess work. Tell them upfront why this meeting is important for them specifically.

Prompt. Always be on time with your meetings as a leader. If you are late, it shows that the meeting is not important. Also be prompt with an end time so your team can manage their schedule better and not create stress. The worst thing is for meetings to drag on as it creates stress for your team as time is usually the biggest thing we must manage in our day.

Present. Your presence as a leader is the biggest gift you can give your team, and it also has become more crucial in the world of distraction we live in. Shut off your device and set the tone for others to do the same. Be focused on the purpose of the meeting and allow for efficiency. If you are distracted yourself, then you cannot set a good example of how you expect your team to behave. The more present you are, the more efficient the meeting can run. I rarely recommend computers at meetings unless it is mandatory to follow along. Anytime someone is behind a screen, you cannot have 100 percent of their attention. If this can't be avoided, then have part of your meeting "tech free" to foster deeper connection and presence.

Personal. I always recommend you do one thing in the meeting that is personal and not about work. It could be a check-in or something that helps everyone personally. A great example of this would be a value-add to them, such as beginning with a mini breath work, stretch, or meditation. Begin with an around-the-table work check-in or a powerful icebreaker to get everybody bonding. One of my favorite icebreakers is: "If you had a superpower, what would it be and why?" The answers are always amazing.

 **EXERCISE: MEETING TEMPLATE BRAINSTORM**

Create a meeting template that you can follow for each meeting. Ideas to include in your template are an opening icebreaker, a key ending takeaway, a group share, and then fill in your agenda.

Plan ahead by booking some months with outside guest speakers and incorporate some wellness and stress-management education. This will set you up for success so you can have effective meetings throughout the year.

KEY POINTS:

- Effective meetings need the five P's: passionate, purposeful, prompt, present, personal.

- Have a content template for your monthly team meetings.

- Make your meetings exciting. They can become a team highlight they look forward to—a reward rather than an obligation.

CHAPTER 19:
ADD WELLNESS TO THE MIX

There have been studies out for years on the importance of having an engaged workforce and how engagement ultimately affects productivity and the bottom line. In fact, for years Gallup surveys have studied what they call "The Wellbeing-Engagement" reciprocal relationship. Historically, when engagement is up in an organization, so is well-being, which has had a positive effect on productivity and lowers burnout. However, during COVID, this relationship changed and created what Gallup called "The Wellbeing-Engagement Paradox of 2020."[22] For the first time, they recorded a divergence in the relationship. During this period, engagement stayed high, but burnout also hit an all-time high, since the recession of 2008. And since then, engagement rates have now moved in the downturn direction and pose great risks to organizations and the global economy.

So, there are a couple things to take from these findings. First, engagement is important and always will be. When your team is engaged, you will have better results in productivity and health and well-being for the individuals and organization. In fact, if you don't have an engaged team, studies show they are also the highest flight risk: 73 percent of actively disengaged employees are on the lookout for new jobs.[23] So, as a leader, it is always a good conscious practice to foster increased engagement.

Second, engagement alone is not enough, as leaders need to also foster a culture around well-being. The paradox of the COVID years shows that we can't just rely on healthy engagement for a healthy organization. We need to prioritize wellness. We need to create a culture around wellness and support our teams with wellness education, including specific tools to handle stress management and burnout.

The right way forward for the conscious leader is to have high levels of engagement from their team with a highly focused culture around fostering wellness. As a heart-centered leader, this will become natural to you because you are more aware of your teams' emotions—you can tell when someone is off right away. You are dialed into your team and can feel the energy when it is out of alignment so you can create pivots or give support when needed rather than wait for a bigger problem to arise and have to react.

A conscious leader practices engagement and wellness and makes it a part of everyday life.

SIMPLE WAYS TO KEEP ENGAGEMENT AT HEALTHY LEVELS:

Connecting with employees

Employee connection and healthy communication is directly linked to healthy engagement. Think about this in any relationship. When one partner is disengaged with the other, the relationship starts to break down. Interaction lessons and meaningful conversations become nonexistent, and the relationship becomes flat and disappointing. This is usually in a relationship when people will put their energy into different things to fill a void; it could be other friends, substances, work, or exercise. In life, we are always drawn toward things that feel good. So, if a relationship doesn't feel good, we will find our focus is looking for other things to give us this satisfaction. It is the same with the employees on your team. They will look in other places or for other jobs if they are not feeling fulfilled. Therefore, check in, ask about personal things, get to know them on a deeper level, and find out what matters most to them. Remember important dates like birthdays. It also means having healthy communication about the goals of the organization by talking about strategic visions and keeping them in the loop.

Healthy feedback

Another way to create healthy engagement is by getting feedback often from your team. Ask them for their thoughts on things, ask them for advice, make them feel part of the company direction and that their voice matters. Find as many ways and as often as possible to get feedback or ask for their opinion. The best part of leading this way is you will also be amazed as to the incredible insights you will get and the different perspectives you could not have seen or thought of on your own. Feedback often makes a dynamic and engaged team.

Be transparent

When I first started out in leadership, I did not understand the importance of transparency. I was taught to only share bits and pieces with the team and to never let them see you have a bad day. I don't agree with this anymore. With healthy transparency, there are two important aspects. Transparency with the organization, such as financial health, direction, goals, and the ups and downs. Then there is transparency from you as an individual. Don't be afraid to show your human side. Let them know if you don't know the answer, but you will find out. It's okay to be up front if you are having a tough moment or day, because they will feel the energy coming off you anyway, so better to get ahead of it rather than them making assumptions, which are always worse. Many times, when the boss is off, it creates great fear in employees because the first thing they assume is it is about them. So be upfront and humanize yourself and your emotions. Be honest.

Have brainstorming sessions

There is nothing more powerful than the building of ideas from a collective group. I always find it magical as to how much brilliance comes out of brainstorming sessions. Our genius builds on some-one else's genius, and it has this compounding effect where the outcome is divine. Look for opportunities to come up with brilliance through brainstorming sessions. I always love to add food or make it a coffee or tea date, so it feels more intimate and caring. As the leader, make sure you encourage input and ideas shared from everyone. You will always have more dominant personalities, but it is important to make everyone feel heard. This is the part about creating psychological safety.

SIMPLE WAYS TO CREATE A CULTURE AROUND WELLNESS:

Be well yourself

There is nothing more inspiring than leading a healthy lifestyle. Move your body daily, eat high energy and whole foods during the work week, drink lots of water, have a daily mindfulness practice, and take breaks.

Invest in workplace wellness

Set aside a budget for wellness training. It is no longer just about job training; as leaders, we now need to be responsible for also giving our employees tools and training around wellness. Have a budget for speakers or wellness trainers to come in and empower your team to take care of themselves with tips on how to build lasting healthy habits, including around the power of the mind and changing ways to lessen stress.

Stress-management tool kits

I can guarantee I would not be able to deal with the daily stressors if I did not have the tools to manage stress and foster my own wellness. One of my favorite things to do is to have the team members share what they do to manage their stress. Get your team to inspire each other and educate each other. This is sharing love and decreasing the stress. The wellness tool kit can be a lifesaver.

Some of my favorites are:

- Breath work
- Meditations
- Essential oils
- Sound therapy
- Light therapy
- Movement
- Forest baths
- Grounding
- EFT or tapping and hypnosis
- Yoga
- Gratitude journaling
- Intention setting
- Cleansing, such as sound, selenite, or palo santo

Wellness breaks

Have wellness breaks as part of your daily routine and company culture. Have group sharing and accountability around this. For instance, in your next morning meeting, get the group to share what they did for their wellness breaks the previous day. This can be anywhere from five to thirty minutes.

Transition times

Schedule transition times between meetings. Back-to-back meetings create burnout. Even if it is a five-minute transition to grab water and coffee or tea, go to the bathroom, step outside and take a breath of fresh air, do a cleansing breath. Transition times are important, so you fuel up throughout the day. Create a culture around this as your company's new normal. Back-to-back meetings are counterproductive and go against our bodies and our minds that need to be refueled.

Healthy boundaries

Don't email your team at 2 a.m. and think it sets a good example. First, if you are doing this, you are setting unrealistic expectations for your team. Second, it never looks good if the boss has to work all hours of the night to get the job done. Unless working on a huge deadline, this should never be a normal work habit. Set healthy boundaries for you and healthy expectations for your team. Work–life balance.

As a leader in today's time when you lead with heart, you will naturally be inspired to ensure a healthy engaged team and a culture around wellness. These two important mindsets will create a more loyal, enthusiastic, positive, and productive team. And when we spend most of our hours in our work environment, nothing is more important than a healthy and happy team.

KEY POINTS:

- Engagement will always be important, but it is not enough to ensure a healthy organization.

- A culture around well-being and educating around health and stress management has become essential.

- Creating this environment must start with you! You set the tone as the leader.

CHAPTER 20:
EVERYONE HAS A ZONE OF GENIUS

One of the most important things to do as a leader is to help guide, cultivate, encourage, foster, grow, and nourish your team's "zone of genius." Gay Hendricks, influential psychologist and best-selling author, coined this phrase in *The Big Leap*[24] to refer to living and working within your full potential. Your zone of genius is that thing you do that you are really good at, that you love, and that feels effortless—it is an extension of you. We all have a zone of genius, including you, and when you tap into what that is, magic happens. We know when we work in our zone of genius because we feel lit up, we feel like we are in flow, we feel like it is easy. Our zone of genius is directly connected to our purpose, and each one of us has a unique purpose.

It took me years to really find my zone of genius. I always knew it was to be a leader, but cultivating and refining what that meant took some years to unpack for me. Most of you reading this now will probably have moments when you know you are in your zone of genius because you take inspired action, things feel easier, and you feel a nudge deep inside that almost guides your actions. It feels like the work you do is an extension of yourself—because it is.

Years ago when I was leading our sales team, our business seemed to suddenly plateau and I wasn't sure why. We weren't bringing in new business, so I looked closely at our sales team and took note of each member's skills. Rather than see each salesperson as having the same skillset, I was able to see each one's strengths and weaknesses.

I then restructured the team so each member would be able to focus on what came more naturally to them, what they excelled at. Some focused on procurement, some focused on client relationship management, and some focused on the details and finalizing contracts. Then our team began to shine because everyone was now working with their strengths rather than with their weaknesses. They were more productive and happier because each was working in their zone.

The opposite is true when we work against our zone of genius.

HOW DO YOU FIND YOUR ZONE OF GENIUS?

Finding your zone of genius requires you to listen to yourself, listen to your body, listen to your emotions and what you are feeling. For many of us, we have turned this volume button all the way down and continued to plow through, even when we hate what we are doing. Sometimes we just need to adjust in our current job, although other times, it might mean moving in a different direction altogether. The important part here is to listen to the inner compass that we all have. If something feels hard or like a constant struggle, that is your body telling you a change is needed, such as an upgrade in either your own mindset or a radical shift in your life. I believe it is always a good idea to do an internal check.

I ENCOURAGE YOU TO DO A HAPPINESS EVALUATION AND ASK YOURSELF:

- Am I happy?
- Do I love what I do?
- What would or could make my situation better?

Not only is it healthy to do this on yourself but also as a regular and positive maintenance program for your team. But it must start with you. Your happiness will be infectious for others around you, and one way to ensure you are happy is if you are working in your own divine flow or zone of genius. The other important thing is to hire people for the things you dislike, because this pulls you out of your zone. And the best part is that there is someone who loves doing the things you don't. My assistant and I always laugh, as we have a huge appreciation for each other. She always says to me, "Julie, I could never do what you do." I love speaking on big stages, while she likes being behind the scenes and thrives on administration. Administrative work gives me hives, and I have such a huge appreciation for her as she frees me up to be in my zone of genius. It is a win-win scenario.

My son came home not long ago and told me that one of the administrative staff at his school had attended one of my workshops. Because of what I'd said about happiness, she changed her job and now is so happy. He said she wouldn't have done this if she wasn't prompted by my talk. It amazes me how we are willing to tolerate so much unhappiness. I found myself doing that for a lot of my life. I never felt like I was able to make the change or that I could give myself permission to follow my heart. For the first time in my life I can honestly say I love what I do, and I am fully in my zone of genius. For me, I am not driven by money but by my purpose and passion. When you can align these two things, your zone of genius will show its face and abundance can come with ease.

 **EXERCISE: PASSION CHECKLIST**

Let's do a quick exercise to check in with purpose and passion. Write down as many things as you can that you're passionate about.

For example, my passions are:

- ✓ Helping people see their true potential
- ✓ Public speaking
- ✓ Coaching individuals and seeing them reach their stretch goals
- ✓ Facilitating retreats
- ✓ Anything to do with wellness
- ✓ Manifestation
- ✓ Yoga
- ✓ Meditation
- ✓ Being active

Now take a look at your list and put a check mark beside the things that you get to do in your job, or maybe in a volunteer position, meaning you are fulfilling these passions with your purpose in life through your work. The key here is to see if you are able to fulfill your passions in your current line of work. If there is nothing on your list that is connected to your passion, then changes need to be made. You are not working in your zone.

The purpose and passion checklist will help to keep you in alignment and be guided by what changes you will need to make in your current situation to be in better alignment with yourself or if a change is needed from your current job or organization.

One thing I will emphatically tell you is it's your birthright to be happy, so never give up your control in making that happen. You are the only one who can decide what that is for you. As a leader, it is important to understand that this is the same for your team and that you can be the happiness guide. You can inspire them to do the inner work and see if their purpose and passion is in alignment. Do not be afraid of the answer because when you build a team that is working in their zone of genius, you will find the results skyrocket with the right healthy environment.

Get them to do the same exercise and guide them to do the inner work. If there are things that they are unhappy with, see if there can be adjustments made to make life better. Sometimes it can be a simple change where they hate parts of their job, but love others, and you can adjust to allow them to work more often in their zone of genius. Just like I reorganized my sales team, companies can benefit from looking at how things operate and adjust and allow for better flow. Sometimes the best way is not the way it has always been done.

KEY POINTS:

- We all have a zone of genius; this is what makes the world go round.

- Find out the parts of your job you love and what other parts you can delegate.

- Do a happiness reorganization on your team. Ask what parts they love and what parts they don't. Where possible, make the shifts.

- We are all meant to be happy, and we all deserve to be happy. Working with your purpose and passion keep you in alignment and make you happy.

CHAPTER 21:
INSPIRATION IS THE KEY

Growing up, I would always study and learn from people I admired on how to be a motivating leader. And it would feel so good when people would compliment me on being motivating. What I have realized over the years is that being a motivating leader is important, but what is powerful is being an inspired leader. Inspiration will have lasting effects whereas motivation can be useful for short bouts of change or feeling fueled. Inspiration comes from the heart whereas motivation comes from the mind. The heart space will always be more powerful because it connects to your center, to your inner self, and to your purpose.

Inspiration is what is needed in the workplace and for our kids at school. For example, we can help give our kids motivation to study for a test. We might even give them a reward for doing well, which might work. But then the next test comes along and without the motivation, the kid might not do the work. Inspiration instead connects them to themselves, which will have a lasting effect. Inspiration connects to why they should want to do well in school. What would that do for them? What doors will it open? What university or college do they want to go to? How would it make them feel to do well?

If your kid is the scholastic type, then these deeper connections to the why will help to motivate them to have the drive come from within. My one child is very motivated to do well in school. He likes the feeling of staying on top of his work, he likes the feeling of getting good marks, and he enjoys school. He cares. This goes deeper than motivation. He is inspired to do well. As much as I would like to take the credit, he really found that inspiration from within. My other child is not as motivated, and it comes and goes. However, when we did the university tours this year, she fell in love with a certain university and could imagine herself being there. It is competitive to get in, and this connection has given her the inspiration to now be more consistent with her studies. She has told me in so many words, "Mom, I will get in; I am going to school there." The dots connected for her. I don't need to motivate her because she gets it and now has the drive within her.

I believe as leaders we can help guide our team or our kids to find inspiration from within.

Sometimes we need shorter bouts of motivation to be able to create a habit or positive lifestyle change that then becomes inspiration from within. For example, I wanted to start walking regularly and I was able to do this for a while, but I could never be consistent. My motivation was my dog was happier with regular walks, but this wasn't enough for me because when I felt lazy, I could just throw her a ball or let her run in our backyard. I would find excuses like it's too cold, I'm too tired, I'm not feeling it today, etc. But then it shifted for me because my friend who lives a few houses down became my walking buddy. Now I felt a deeper why. My why was because we would have great talks, so it filled my emotional cup to go on walks. Yes, my dog was thrilled, and I was happy too. Then I started to feel better in my clothing, which made me feel more confident. And I began to feel more energetic, which made me feel more youthful and productive. I started to get addicted to the feel-good action of walking. I now crave it. My body tells me to go, and the excuses are very infrequent. I am inspired versus motivated to walk. My deeper purpose of walking is the connection to self, my friend, my dog, and nature. And it creates the mental shift I need in my busy day. It is no longer just a walk.

As leaders, if we can connect to the bigger purpose of why our teams work for us or the company, why they like or want their jobs, and what their dreams are, then we can connect to the bigger purpose of their jobs, which will go way beyond just going to work to get a paycheck. It will connect to inspiration.

We can pull that out of our team by asking some key questions:

- "Why did you apply for this job in the first place?"
- "Why is that important to you?"
- "Why do you like working here?"
- "Why do you like that?"
- "Why is that important to you?" And so on . . .

Keep asking the deeper questions about why, and you will realize that the core nugget that is behind inspiration is usually being in service to others.

As humans, no matter what we do, we are motivated by being in service to others because it feels good. And I know that if you dig deep enough with the whys, it will always get to the core of acts of service. As I mentioned in the previous chapter, we all have our zones of genius. Every single one of us. The key is following the intuitive nudges to discover yours. When you are working from your place of genius, work will be fun because you have connected to your purpose. I was thinking about a good friend of ours who is a brilliant lawyer and handles complicated cases. He could easily retire, but he keeps working because he loves it. I was also thinking how much I would absolutely hate what he does, but I am in awe of how good he is at it. He connected to his zone of genius, which connected to his purpose in life. He does not live a motivated life but an inspired life. That is why for him, it is not about reaching retirement but enjoying what you do no matter what age. You might choose a slower-paced work life later, but there has to be a better reality than working in the now to live for the future. This philosophy does not make sense.

We recently had one of our closest friends pass away three years before retirement. It was painful because his death was so sudden, but what gave me peace was how much he loved his life, his job. He was an electrician who found his purpose. He was always happy to be in service to people, and he got great satisfaction in doing his work and seeing the end results or solving a complex installment at work. One would say how sad that he died just short of retirement if he didn't love his work or if he was working just to be able to retire. My friend's life was a huge reminder to really enjoy your life, enjoy what you do and live from a place of inspiration because that is connected to your true self. This is what makes the world go around.

Have you ever sat back in awe just thinking about all the different jobs that exist in the world? And how there is always someone to fill every different and unique job? One person decides they want to be an electrician, another a lawyer, one a nurse, one an engineer, one a healer, and on and on. Ultimately, we were all led to exactly where we are right now, and it is not an accident how we got here. Now, if you are reading this and saying well, I am not happy in what I am doing, that is okay. Find out why you are not happy and what would make you happy instead. Focus on what would make you happy and change your antenna to attract more happiness. You will find the inspiration to make a change if that is what you need in your career, or to have a healthy boundary or to speak to your boss about a change or to find the missing link as to what is needed on your team.

Whatever situation you are in, the key to living an inspired life and to becoming an inspirational leader is to first connect to your truth as to why you are doing what you do, what got you into this in the first place, and what ultimately lights you up. Remember, there is purpose in all of us. We might have to take a few twists and turns to get there, but I always believe that those twists and turns are us figuring out more about what we do want and what we truly are meant to do. All our past and present experiences are to discover more about who we are and what lights us up. And as a leader, the best way to create that unstoppable, highly inspired team is by helping them connect back to their deeper why.

LEADERSHIP BEST PRACTICES TO CREATE AN INSPIRED TEAM:

- Book time with each of your team members or leaders to have a connection to your WHY session.
- Ask layers of why questions to get them connected to the deeper meaning of why they work for you or the company.

- Ask them what drives them, what gets them inspired.

- Connect the dots back to the company's overall mission (most of the times, it is connected to a place of service, which will also connect back to the individual's deeper why).

- By connecting these dots from the company mission to the individual mission, it will light a flame.

- Ask about future career aspirations and set them up on a path to reach those with some key benchmark goals and guidance on how.

- Do these check-ins every six months to a year. This is different from an annual review, but you could add this section into that. However, it is so impactful that it could be a meeting on its own.

- Taking this time to connect with everyone will also create a deeper bond and rapport with your team.

- This is heart-centered leadership, and this will show up in performance, I guarantee.

NOTE: If this feels awkward at first that is perfectly okay. Remember, these are the deeper questions that most people are not used to answering or have even given themselves permission to explore. This will become easier and is an amazing thing to do as a leader because you are inspiring them to connect deeper to themselves. This type of deeper connection to self and their why will also help to smooth out the times when you are in challenges. They help with loyalty and engagement because they can take themselves above the current drama and connect back to why they are here.

LEADING WITH THE HEART MEANS BEING INSPIRATIONAL

Inspiration versus Motivation	
Lead from the heart	Lead from the head
Pulls forward	Pushes from behind
Long lasting	Short bursts
Is in flow	Takes effort
Brings joy	Creates bouts of satisfaction

KEY POINTS:

- Being an inspired leader will create the biggest and most lasting impact.

- Inspiration comes from the heart and is always connected to your deeper why.

- When we connect to our deeper why, it will act like an anchor keeping us stable in the rough waters or the tougher times.

- When we take time to lead with inspiration, we connect deeper on an emotional level with our team members, which creates more connection to the company and generates loyalty because it allows teams to feel cared for and heard.

- Although this might feel awkward at first, it will set you apart from other leaders because this is true heart-centered leadership.

CHAPTER 22:
BRING IT BACK TO YOU

The only thing we are truly in control of is our own thoughts, reactions, words, and energy we emit daily. The most power we have in creating impact around us as individuals and especially as leaders is our vibration or energy. So, the good news is understanding that we can only control ourselves, which means we can take our power back. The other important thing is understanding that when we work ourselves up the emotional scale with love, we will undoubtedly create ripples of greatness. We will create our biggest impact.

TAKE YOUR POWER BACK AND SHINE!

So, it is simple, really; it always comes back to Self, You, and I. The power is in your internal world to create the change you want to see in your external world. Go to your thoughts and the internal story you are telling yourself to see the reel change around you. Stop hoping, praying, or wishing for better results around you, just start to believe in them and feel them in your energetic field. See the good in people; see what they are capable of. And always get yourself back into alignment by asking one simple question of yourself: Am I acting from a place of love, kindness, and support?

In any situation, even the most difficult, you will be able to prosper and get to the other side with a far better outcome when you operate from love, kindness, and support.

It is your time to shine. There has never been more need on the planet than right now for you to step into your light, to own your power, and to shine bright. The world is ready for your light. The world is ready for your truth. The world is ready for that magnificent power that lies deep within you.

You already are a leader; you were born one. When you choose to lead with your heart you will be a magnet for people. Your team will feel inspired, and it will feel easy for you. You will not feel like you must work so hard or prove yourself in any way because you will already know you are worthy—you just need to be fully you.

If I could go back to my younger self as a leader, I would have repeated this as a mantra until it was coded in my cells: "I am enough. I am capable. I am a leader. I lead with love."

The most powerful thing we can do is love ourselves first, heal our triggers, and then let love take over. You will not need to prove yourself because you will have an inner connection to self and an inner knowing of your greatness. And you will be able to help others see the inner greatness within them, ripples and ripples of light and love. That is who you are, and I believe your time has now come to step into your innate power and shine.

One thing I know for sure is that if I could change some of my old programming that said, "Life is hard, I must sacrifice for work, etc." to new programming that says, "I am capable and smart and have everything I need," then you can too! I can vouch for how much lighter and brighter you'll feel. We each have the key to our own liberation. We don't need anyone else—it is within us all. Your job as a leader is to unlock that liberation within you first and then to help others see it within themselves.

Love, light, and prosper,

Julie

ACKNOWLEDGMENTS

Life can be magical. We are magical beings—I believe this from the depths of my soul. We can achieve whatever our hearts desire. And what turns this into rocket fuel is someone else believing in your dreams and aspirations—when others are happy for your happiness and accomplishments. I feel so blessed to have my circle of people in my life who do this for me.

This book was an interesting experience for me as I thought it would be so much easier the second time around. With my second book, I faced more challenges than with my first one, so I needed the help of my people even more to get this book completed.

Thank you again to my incredible publishing team at fEMPOWER Publications. Sabrina, your coaching and support was instrumental to me in making this happen. Christine, you are always so calming and reassuring when I need it most. Kelly, thank you for stepping in and being an exceptional editor that worked from the heart. And a big thank you to Michelle always bringing her artistic genius to the process.

My Positive Change team. Thank you for your support and belief and patience with me to get this book done. Susan, you are a rock, and I am so grateful to you.

My soul sisters at Hypnosishealers.ca. I am so blessed to have you in my life in so many ways. You allow me to stretch and get comfortable about owning my big audacious dreams. You cheer me on and always believe in me. Jenn, thank you for your magical wisdom and your help, especially toward the end to hit my deadline. Your messages of inspiration lit me up and the words began to fly out of me. Robin and Hellen, thank you for always believing in me and being my calm force by my side.

To my hubby and kids: Thank you for your patience when I was grumpy at times, feeling the pressure looming of reaching my deadlines. I love you to the moon and back a million times.

The best gift we can give anyone is believing in them. Sometimes it is the inspiration we need to act and get it done.

Live your dream-filled life. I believe in you!

Julie

REFERENCES

1. "Feeling the Burn: 96% of Managers in Canada Say Their Staff are Experiencing Some Degree of Burnout," Newswire, August 20, 2019. https://www.newswire.ca/news-releases/feeling-the-burn-96-of-managers-in-canada-say-their-staff-are-experiencing-some-degree-of-burnout-827317889

2. "Canadians willing to take new job for less pay if it means more mental health support: study," Global News, January 29, 2020. https://globalnews.ca/news/6477531/morneau-she-pell-mental-health-workplace-study/#:~:text=In%20addi-tion%2C%20the%20study%20suggested,support%20for%20their%20well%2Dbeing

3. "Here's Why Your Parents Stayed at the Same Job for 20 Years," The Associated Press, May 10, 2016. https://fortune.com/2016/05/10/baby-boomers-millennials-jobs/

4. "How to Tap with Jessica Ortner: Emotional Freedom Technique Informational Video," accessed October 10, 2024. https://www.youtube.com/watch?v=pAclBdj20ZU; "Shift from Hard to Easy for the Heart-Centered Leader," accessed October 10, 2024. https://www.youtube.com/watch?v=Qg2LTrQyyp0

5. "Guided Loving Healing Heart Meditation," accessed October 10, 2024. https://www.youtube.com/c/juliecass @Juliecass (for meditative videos)

6. Hypnosis Healers: https://hypnosishealers.ca/

7. "State of the Global Workplace," Gallup, accessed October 10, 2024. https://www.gallup.com/workplace/349484/state-of-the-global-workplace.aspx

8. "2023 Work in America Survey," American Psychological Association, accessed October 10, 2024. https://www.apa.org/pubs/reports/work-in-america/2023-workplace-health-well-being

9. "Mental health at work," World Health Organization, September 2, 2024. https://www.who.int/news-room/fact-sheets/detail/mental-health-at-work

10. "Employers need to focus on workplace burnout: Here's why," American Psychological Association, May 12, 2023. https://www.apa.org/topics/healthy-workplaces/workplace-burnout

11. "2024 Edelman Trust Barometer: Trust at Work," Edelman, accessed October 16, 2024. https://www.edelman.com/trust/2024/trust-barometer/special-report-trust-at-work

12. "Disengagement Persists Among U.S. Employees," Gallup, updated September 11, 2023. https://www.gallup.com/workplace/391922/employee-engagement-slump-continues.aspx

13. "The Cost of Poor Leadership on Your Revenue and Culture," GBS Corporate, July 13, 2017. https://www.gbscorporate. com/blog/the-cost-of-poor-leadership-on-your-revenue-and-culture

14. "This Fixable Problem Costs U.S. Businesses $1 Trillion," Gallup, March 13, 2019. https://www.gallup.com/work-place/247391/fixable-problem-costs-businesses-trillion.aspx

15. "In New Workplace, U.S. Employee Engagement Stagnates," Gallup, January 23, 2024. https://www.gallup.com/work-place/608675/new-workplace-employee-engagement-stag-nates.aspx

16. "Alarming Burnout Leadership Statistics Revealed, Costing Companies Billions," WifiTalents, Updated August 6, 2024. https://wifitalents.com/statistic/leadership-burnout/#:~:-text=96%25%20of%20senior%20leaders%20are,three%20 years%20due%20to%20burnout.

17. "10 Gallup Reports to Share with Your Leaders," January 4, 2019. https://www.gallup.com/workplace/245786/gallup-re-ports-share-leaders-2019.aspx

18. "Psychological Safety and Learning Behavior in Work Teams," Administrative Science Quarterly, Sage Journals, June 1999. https://journals.sagepub.com/doi/abs/10.2307/2666999

19. "What Job Seekers Really Think About Your Diversity and Inclusion Stats," Glassdoor, June 12, 2021. https://www.glass-door.com/employers/blog/diversity/

20. "Managers Impact Our Mental Health More Than Doctors, Therapists—and Same as Spouses," UKG Workforce Institute, January 24, 2023. https://www.ukg.ca/about-us/newsroom/managers-impact-our-mental-health-more-doctors-therapists-and-same-spouses

21. "Team dynamics: Five keys to building effective teams," Google, updated June 2023. https://www.thinkwithgoogle.com/intl/en-emea/future-of-marketing/management-and-culture/five-dynamics-effective-team/

22. "The Wellbeing-Engagement Paradox of 2020," Gallup, March 13, 2021. https://www.gallup.com/workplace/336941/wellbeing-engagement-paradox-2020.aspx

23. "In New Workplace, U.S. Employee Engagement Stagnates," Gallup, January 23, 2024. https://www.gallup.com/work-place/608675/new-workplace-employee-engagement-stag-nates.aspx

24. Hendricks, Gay, PhD, *The Big Leap*, 2009, Harper Collins.

At fEMPOWER, we help thought leaders and creative entrepreneurs capture their vision in the form of nonfiction books, journals, workbooks, affirmation cards, and personal growth products.

Our mission is to help our authors grow and scale a platform far beyond the book, protect their soul's work, and turn their message into a legacy!

www.fempower.pub

 @fempower.pub

www.ingramcontent.com/pod-product-compliance
Lightning Source LLC
Chambersburg PA
CBHW051311120626
46547CB00015B/2193